The Cats WHO LOVE(D) ME

& The One

WHO DOESN'T

The Cats WHO LOVE(D) ME & The One WHO DOESN'T

Joyce FitzGerald Galloway

CITI OF BOOKS

CITIOFBOOKS, INC.
3736 Eubank NE Suite A1
Albuquerque, NM 87111-3579
www.citiofbooks.com
Hotline: 1 (877) 389-2759
Fax: 1 (505) 930-7244

Ordering Information:

Quantity sales. Special discounts are available on quantity purchases by corporations, associations, and others. For details, contact the publisher at the address above.

Printed in the United States of America.

ISBN-13:   Softcover   978-1-962366-58-8
            eBook   978-1-962366-59-5
            Hardback   978-1-962366-72-4

Library of Congress Control Number: 2023919068

To GEHOVAH the Creator of
All and to All Those who love, respect and appreciate that
Creation

For Eddie

Preface

You will not go very far into my story before the statement I am about to make will likely brand me a liar, but the truth is: I never wanted a cat— any cat, regardless of how cute, cuddly, or affectionate. This is not to say I didn't love cats. Since early childhood experiences with my mother's cats, they have always appealed to me and have drawn my attention and interest, but my idea of having a cat or more was dependent on a perfect circumstance—a house with an ample yard and high-enough fence or wall so they could feel as if they were roaming freely while keeping safe from harm; enough rooms so they could have their space and I could have mine; and a reliable sitter I could call on short notice so that I could pursue my desires for impulsive or distant travel. Since this situation didn't develop until I was well into adulthood, even the thought of going out to get a cat did not cross my mind. As it turned out, it didn't have to.

For the seventeen years that we spent in an apartment where no pets were allowed, my involvement with cats was restricted to strays. My hometown is the one about which some readers may recall fictional Sergeant Mike Barnett announcing during the credits of a '50s TV show that "There are eight million stories in the Naked City—this has been one of them." I was a citizen of the Naked City and developed a sincere inner belief that if any-thing on four feet was cold, hungry, lost, injured, or all of the above, it would wait for all 7,999,999 to pass by before making an appearance in front of me. Despite a great amount of heartache and inconvenience, which may perhaps fill another volume, my involvement was, to a point, largely detached. These creatures, that occasionally included dogs, were not my daily friends and companions. Throughout the centuries, cats have maintained the universal reputation of being distant, independent, aloof, moody, and totally wrong to depend on for affection, loyalty, companionship, tenderness, and compassion. It is supposed to be well known that cats simply do not possess these characteristics, and if that is what one wants and needs from a pet, one had better get a dog. These known "facts" may even make the title of this book questionable. ("Surely she must mean the cats she's loved.") My love for cats will most definitely shine through, as who could not reciprocate what has been given to me, but it is the overwhelming devotion that I have received from my cats that enables me to dare any dog who ever existed to top or even match that gift. I once read that no creature is dead for as long as it is alive in your memory. If this is so, it is inconsequential that most of the cats about which I write have long returned to the dust. If memory is what counts, for as long as I live, each one of these cats will be a part of me.

The Cottage

It sits high on a bluff overlooking the ever-changing North Atlantic. Three years have gone by since I locked the door for the last time. Even though it is right next door, and it is still unsold, and I still have the key, I cannot go in there. Deep into shadowy nights, I go there all the time—in my dreams. It always shines with the glow of new paint, widened windows, a carpet here, a staircase there, and always there are more rooms—new levels in which to stretch out and I expand and drink ' in the sun-dappled, salty ocean below.

As each new day fills with light, the cottage is the first sight out of our upstairs window facing the west. The lure pulls me on moonless nights when I come home to my own house, strategically lit to give the appearance of occupancy, especially on those nights when my husband is at work and I am coming home alone. *It* sits alone in the dark, waiting for me, and always, for a moment, my instinct is to go there. But I dare not, because I know that if I do, THEY will be there, each and every one of them. The sad longing to reach out for them, to feel their breaths against my face, to hold them again, to relive just one of the days when they were all alive, when happiness was complete… would hurl me into a pit of melancholy.

And, after all, many of them are with us yet, in the new house, and a new life; and I sometimes muse as to whether or not this place will haunt me as well— when today becomes the past, and these, too, are gone.

Oceans and Shores

It was the winter of 1967 that found us in Cork, the bustling, second largest city of the Emerald Isle. With a young child to raise, as well as parents well along into their golden years, the Naked City had become a bit too naked for us. So, we had returned to the land of my father's birth for a working respite of indefinite length, that small isle of infinite enchantment nestled in the North Atlantic, where gales from the west kiss jagged rocks and mist-covered mountains meet barriers of sand that separate them from the sea.

Summer days when the lingering blue and purple twilight took their time to fade into brief nights had been gradually replaced with mid-afternoon darkness and an unfriendly, penetrating cold that sharply contrasted with the warmth of the people.

It was on such an evening that I wrestled with myself. Should or should I not venture out into the freezing wind and rain? The walk would be long—up the hill on Evergreen Road, past the foreboding ruins of the Red Abbey, down a steep incline, eventually winding my way across the Lee, to a Bible study being held on the other side of the river.

"Down the road a bit" has an entirely different interpretation in Europe than back in "The States." "Go out," "go to bed," "go out," tossing in my head long enough, "go out" won out. "No one else is going" did not succeed in changing my mind, but it may as well have because I never made it to the Grand Parade.

Nearly at the foot of Nicholas Hill, added to the sounds of the night, was a wail so pitiful that I can still hear it as vividly as if it were only yesterday. Trying to climb out of the rain-filled gutter was a soaking-wet and terribly frightened tiger kitten. She clung to and clawed me as I tucked her inside my coat and made the long climb back up the hill.

With her safely inside, after drying, calming, and feeding the kitten, our delayed reaction was bewilderment at being pet owners for the first time since my childhood. This feeling was quickly replaced with the old familiar sense of completeness that comes to those willing to make room for an animal in their lives. Anyone who has had a kitten knows there is nothing to compare with its antics. The name of the estate that housed our flat was Ivy Lawn. There was no ivy, but as the door in the wall opened from the cobblestone city street, the expanse of green lawn with vines overhanging arbors along the garden path lived up to the loveliness that its title suggests. It was here that our newly found "Penny" chased butterflies as she developed from a lonely waif into a loving, sensitive, and caring cat.

There had been some dark, stormy days in my own life days when I had felt caught up as in a whirlwind, spun around like a boat in a storm; and when it was over, Penny was like the ray of sun that lit up calm waters. I will always look back on her as a badly needed special gift.

As my story will amply reflect, each and every cat that was to come into our lives would attach itself to one or the other of us: one to my father, two to my husband, a couple to my mother, and the great majority to me. Penny was unmistakably my daughter Jeannine's cat.

Jeannine's hearing was perfect; so was her ability to tune out at will anything that she did not want to listen to especially if it was coming from me. Sometimes I felt it necessary to turn up my own volume. So it was that on any occasion when I could be even loosely described as yelling at my daughter; if Penny was on hand, she jumped immediately between us, taking her stand in defense of the child. This action never failed to quiet, not only my voice, but also my spirit. It would have been easy to push the cat aside, but there was something very touching about the small creature's appeal to the calm and reasonable woman inside of me.

It was toward the end of our second year in Cork that we began to get an inkling of the resurrection of "The Troubles" in the North, which in time the entire world would become painfully aware, remaining so for the next twenty years, and which have, until this day, remained largely unresolved.

Although it was by far mostly confined to Ulster, the occasional report of a threat here or there in the Republic made us, if not afraid, certainly alert to what turn of events the future might hold and how it might affect us.

Every upstanding Irishman or Irishwoman decried the violence of the IRA, denouncing support of its very existence. No one upheld the bloodshed, especially of the uninvolved innocents, those who, as in all wars, are so often victims—the women and the children.

These sentiments did not, however, prevent the popularity of the song of the day, "I'm off to join the IRA—I'm off tomorrow morn. . . . So it's off to Dublin in the green, in the green . . ." invariably produced a gleam in the eye and a lilt in the step and was never far from the lips of young and old alike.

As sympathizers with all who suffer from injustice in any form—earth wide, we had no political persuasions; this was not our battle. They were too kind to make us feel as such, but we were outsiders.

We knew we would not be there permanently. It had never been our intention. Thus, when the letter arrived from across the sea, our answer was "yes" before we even finished reading the invitation it contained. It would be nice to think that everyone has a friend who, no matter what the circumstances, is always there for you when your need is greatest. While we did not feel in any danger, un-easiness grew with uncertainty.

Madelyn Day, cherished friend for a lifetime, was at a crossroads in her life. She wondered if we would like to stay a while with her in Massachusetts as she considered some weighty decisions, at the same time providing us a train station, so to speak, while we looked over schedules and destinations to determine which course our own lives would take. We had not even thought about asking anyone for such temporary refuge, and here it was provided for us.

Tickets were purchased for a sailing the following September. I came home one evening in July to find a new kitten in the flat. Jeannine and some other youngsters had found it at the entrance of a nearby factory, closed for the day. Its fur gray and black striped, its eyes still blue; and unlike the staid, bewildered Penny, it was full of bounce, energy, and every other form of cuteness to be found in a baby cat. But, whatever in the world were we going to do with it? To bring the new kitten with us on a seven-day Atlantic crossing was as unthinkable as leaving the older one behind.

Neighbors on our street had all the animals that they were able to handle. An impulsive call to the vet on Western Road who had spayed Penny could not have been more timely. She had friends in the country whose twenty-year-old cat had been put to sleep the day before. They were heartbroken, and they asked her to keep her eye out for a new kitten. They didn't care if it was male or female. Their only stipulation: that it be beautiful.

We were able to fill the bill. "It" turned out to be a female they named "Trix." Having had her only a few days, we were surprised at how difficult it was to let her go. We would not have dreamed what a large space one so small could leave in our lives—or how empty the flat would seem. We never visited Trix in her new home, but reports told us she was well loved and the thrill of her new owners' lives. Last heard, she waited on the gatepost every night for the man's arrival when she would jump down and ride with him into the house.

As our days in Ireland were winding to a close, we reflected that our time there had been satisfying and happy. We were glad to be bringing with us a living memento.

Penny was not an easy cat to travel with. As much as I loved her and tried to protect her from anything that might cause her fright or harm, there was a trace of sadness in her little soul that never completely left her. It reminded me, not of the people who are known for their sunny nature, but of their land itself from which she came. It is in the mountains and the clouds, the fields and the valleys that all the sorrow that has made up the history of that small country still lives. The land itself can be felt bleeding—and weeping— tears that have no connection to the gentle daily rains that keep it lush and green.

As on the night I found her, Penny cried along every inch of the twenty-two mile road that wound along the River Lee to the sea. Her quarters on the ship were superb, as was its menu. No scraps or canned food for these pampered pets. Only the best of beef, poultry, and fresh fish. It is no wonder that they looked down their noses at us humans as if we were peasants. This was our first experience with animal snobs. Our Penny did not fit in with them; we kept her with us in our cabin whenever possible.

I had heard of the emotions inspired by the Lady in the Harbor. I saw her every day during all the years of my life in New York. She had meant nothing to me then; she would mean nothing now. We were not among the "huddled masses yearning to breathe free." I wasn't even sure I would bother going up on deck, but I wanted to see the Verrazano-Narrows Bridge, completed in our absence. The sun had not yet risen as we sailed underneath, so only the lights could be distinguished. We lay in the Lower Harbor for what seemed hours before proceeding up the bay. Then, there she was, standing straight out of the pink haze that hung over the water.

I was unprepared for the impact that the sight of her would have on me. She did not proclaim freedom or opportunity or any man's philosophy to me. She was a familiar figure welcoming us home. Madelyn and her fiancé Charlie met us at the pier. The family and Penny with them left immediately for their five-hour drive to New England. I had to keep my city's sizzling sidewalks under my feet for a few days. Another friend was there for me, and my first ride over the new bridge was exhilarating.

Two days later, I left home once more, this time on a bus for Boston, which I had passed through only twice before in my life. Nor would I linger this time as I proceeded to my final destination.

Hough's Neck, pronounced as in *how*. Not even the Bostonians whom I approached for directions had heard of it. When I finally reached it after a trolley, a train, and two bus rides, I could see why. Even at night I could feel the enchantment that daylight revealed to be a place suspended in a long-ago time--scene after scene materialized as if from Currier and Ives—a place to be drifted into from a hot-air balloon or a magic carpet, a land of soaring gulls, blue seas, tall grass, intimate coves, sandy beaches, wide marshes—of purple ice and blinding snow, of picket fences and roses. To live here is to become a Necker, and to be a Necker is to be part of a community that is as tight knit and caring as you would expect to find only in a world of make-believe.

We stayed with Madelyn for a month and found ourselves to be in the right place at the right time. There was a house behind hers, facing the ocean, looking to be the right size for our needs, but it was occupied. Early in November, it was unexpectedly vacated. "Would you like to rent it?" asked the landlord. Would we! Where else would we find a full, two-storied cottage with a view that a millionaire would die for? An old-fashioned school was a two-minute walk along the dike; accessibility to the city jobs was easy.

Roads in the Neck are narrow and winding. Bay View Avenue curves high around the bay. Large homes with wide verandas hug the cliff. Our cottage had originally been built for the beach season only, but what it lacked in amenities was made up for in charm. I believe the air that sweeps in from the bay to be the sweetest and freshest on earth. Wild roses grow profusely on "our" cliff, as well as on hundred-foot "suicide hill," which drops sharply to the sea from Great Hill, rising high above the ocean where two bays meet at the very end of the peninsula. From the hill can be seen the thirty islands of Boston Harbor (some with names as intriguing as Sheep, Grape, Raccoon, Moon, and Nut, which adjoins the Neck beyond the hill).

Life in the Neck was to be one of never-ending delights of sight and sound. Penny settled in with the rest of us. Hers to enjoy were the park and the fields of wild flowers bordering the beach. Her favorite spots were the roof of the shed and the overhanging willow tree in the yard next door.

As when we moved to Ireland, this was another first. This time our first experience living in another region of the United States, outside of New York City and weekends in the New Jersey countryside. Because of the similarity of its rolling green farmland to the latter, County Cork seemed more like an extension of what we knew as home. Accustomed as we were to my father's brogue, we barely noticed Irish accents.

Massachusetts, on the other hand, spoke a language that we would have to learn to understand, if not adopt. Still disputed are whether your morning drink is CAWFFEE or CAAFFEE, whether your mother's sister is your ANT or your AWNT, or if we come from NEW YAWK or NEW YOCK.

We expected life here to be an adjustment. Our first year was an initiation to New England weather. ("If you don't like it, wait for ten minutes and it will change.")

Although the other members of my family are not, I am a winter person, and I gloried in the frigid temperatures and the tons of swirling and drifting snow. Our spot on the coast is one from which we can experience nature in all of its changing costumes.

That winter's mantle of white was put on in November and remained, at least in part, through the months to come. The solidly frozen bay was a new phenomenon, one I have never tired of, especially on those days when I am home early enough to watch the sun set and cast its reflection on the snow-covered ice, as the late afternoon becomes a rose-colored world.

Despite a few hurricanes in my New York childhood, with our houses well protected from the battering gales, we soon came to realize we had never really experienced high winds before. Here we had full exposure to the moods of the North Atlantic. Tucked neatly behind a portion of Bay View Avenue, Chapel Street is a short, private road, dead-ending in front of the cottage at the top of the cliff. A few yards to the east, immediately in front of the house in which we now live, there is a *grassy* embankment sloping down to a hollow, which appears to have been scooped out by the hands of a giant. Beyond is the beach, nestled into a cove, and the dike, built to hold back the overflow of the sea.

It is through this hollow that the wind roars, sounding like a freight train, determined with all its worth to destroy whatever lies in its path. I do not remember if it was the noise or the shaking of the cottage that first awoke us, as we cowered in our beds, watching in the dim light from the street lamp as overhead lights shook, objects on dressers danced, and the cottage braced itself in defiance of being swept onto the bay.

The next day, questioning Madelyn whether there had been an earthquake, she laughed. "You'll get used to it."

Never.

Then I recalled how during the first week of a job in a company sharing a border with Newark Airport, I had dived under my desk at the noise and shaking of a plane taking off. Deafening, frightening . . . in time routine, eventually unnoticed. So it went that year in the cottage.

Directly across the street, the house that faced ours had been built into the cliff and bore the worst brunt of the wind. In it was a couple whose family had grown and gone. They lived with only the company of their freckle-faced dog and a large black male cat. "Toodles is his name. But we never let him in the house."

Fine when it was warm and dry. But to sleep in peace knowing a creature you took responsibility for was freezing outside your door?

I doubted if their furniture or rugs were of any greater value than ours. It was not as if there were a garage or a barn, so it was no wonder that when the cold set in, Toodles looked elsewhere for shelter—with us.

He moved in with the ease of a long-lost family member who had no lack of confidence in the certainty of his welcome.

Toodles became my father's cat and was the light of the last years of his life. We now had two cats, male and female; it seemed just right.

Two years later, we needed a vacation—a real vacation, not just a day here or there as time permitted. As in Ireland, when not working, like tourists, we took all the one-day bus tours available to acquaint ourselves with our new locale. We had worked hard to establish our lives with I keeping expenses under control. It was time for a reward. What better way than with a relaxing ocean voyage, one where all we needed to be concerned with was appropriate clothing for the cities that we would visit rather than household items and a frightened cat.

We were to be gone for a month—close to three weeks in London, which we had not really explored when living in Ireland, and another in Paris, which we had not seen at all. When I said good-bye to the cats, Toodles was affectionate as usual. Penny licked my face intently for five to ten minutes. I had to break away from her. My father had announced that his traveling days were over and his choice was to stay behind with friends in New York. The rest of us sailed on a July morning, on the *France* bound for Southampton.

Cram-filled with castles and ruins, museums, art, culture, history we were ready to return to life in our new home.

Nothing could have prepared us for the deadly plague that had lain beneath the surface, waiting until our departure before raising its ugly head.

Among the first words to greet us on disembarking were, "Your cat died."

"Which one?"

"The female. They are trying to save the *male.*"

Whatever in the world had happened? Both cats had been in perfect condition as we left them boarded in the care of a highly recommended vet whose quarters were as clean and cozily homelike as anything we could have hoped to find. My questions came faster than I could think or they could be answered.

When my head cleared, the facts were presented as far as they were known; the rest we pieced together. We had never lived near a beach before. It is possible we had never heard of sand fleas; there had been no reason to be concerned about them. Penny and Toodles had been at the vet's for a few days when the flea eggs unknowingly carried with them hatched, draining the cats of their lifeblood more quickly than they could be destroyed.

That the eggs had been picked up in the Neck there was no doubt. Six other cats in our immediate area were dead. Madelyn's Siamese, Phaedra, was very sick, but she, like Toodles, pulled through. I could not comprehend what happened and never did until fifteen years later when the fleas came back en masse, but that time we were ready. No cat of ours would ever die in such a way again.

Toodles performed no unusual stunts or feats. The only time that he gave us any cause for worry was years later on the early morning in March when we let him out and he failed to return. With the exception of an occasional visit to his former home, he could always be found at our front gate. We had come to cherish him; and since his comings and goings were so predictable, we questioned if there had been foul play. It was with sad hearts that we kept our eyes ever open for any sign of him.

I decided that to cancel a planned trip to Charleston would be useless in bringing him back. It was also useless in taking my mind off him. Dogwood and magnolias did nothing to blot out the pain that I carried with me. Home again, after the third week, we had come to grips with our loss—when in the dim light of a chilly morning, I happened to be sitting at the rear bedroom window, chin on the sill, when there came into view the outline of a thin black cat weakly climbing onto the roof.

Could it be? It was! We couldn't imagine how far he had traveled or what he had run into along the way, but Toodles was home! We never knew for sure, but I always guessed he had fallen asleep in the back of a pick-up truck frequently parked on Chapel Street. When the owner drove off, Toodles likely started out on the ride and jumped off at some point, who knows where, lost and disoriented. But all that really mattered was that he was back with us, hungry, but safe, and happy to be home.

Fluffy and Her Family

It was about a year before losing Penny that we first became aware of Miss Fluffy Healy. A huge-eared pointed-chinned elflike kitten with the tail of a squirrel began appearing on our first-floor roof and inviting herself in the bedroom window. At the time, two cats seemed to be our limit; besides, she belonged to neighbors and had a fine home. Though we did nothing to encourage the visits, they became so frequent that every time we opened a door or a window, in would swish Miss Fluff, adorned with a pink or blue ribbon and smelling of perfume. Jeannine would carry her home, but this was not welcomed by her owners who asked that we allow her to come by herself.

The visits continued up to and beyond Penny's death, and we began to look forward to that tail bouncing in and out of our daily routine, although Fluffy's fickleness caused increasing irritation on the part of our neighbors. One cold day, there was a knock on our back door and a pained expression on the face of the young girl who held Fluffy in her arms. "She's pregnant, and my mother says you can have her." "Thanks," was all I could say. I knew that if I said anything else, Fluffy would end up in the pound. Also, she would help to heal our sore hearts and fill the vacancy our little Irish waif had left in our lives.

Fluffy waddled as she grew plump, and I believe this was due as much to contentment as to her pregnancy. She seldom went beyond the back door, and out of the yard only to follow one of us down the street. Inside, there was no place to curl up but on one of our laps.

This was our first experience with a pregnant cat, and the question of how many bundles of joy we would have to find homes for was never far from our minds and sometimes made our hearts sink. We comforted ourselves with the thought that sometimes there were only two or three kittens to a litter. A lesser concern was where the new family was to arrive, and to that end we made "nests" of boxes and blankets in every conceivable spot.

As her time drew near, her affection expanded along with her middle. I went to bed, as usual, sleeping on my back, the night of February 11, 1970, a night remembered for its cold and snow, as well as Fluffy's presentation to us of her family. I woke up to a bearing down on my stomach. I felt Fluffy there; but when I touched her, she let out a yelp as the first kitten emerged on my thighs. The household awakened, the lights were turned on, and I gently nestled her to my right side and held her closely as the next six babies made their way into the world. I don't believe a more beautiful batch of kittens was ever born. It has now been twenty-two years, and I stand by that assessment. They were healthy, lively, pretty, cute, long-haired, short-haired, curious, and bad.

We found an enormous box for them to nurse and frolic in, and before long the favorite game was to leap over the side. We had early decided that we would not allow ourselves to become attached to any of the kittens, that they must all leave, and then Fluffy would be spayed and she and the threatened Toodles would be our only cats. This "decision" was based on information given us that the kittens should stay with us for ten weeks.

Through word of mouth, good homes were lined up for four of them, one each for Madelyn's little girls who lived immediately behind us, and one each to two work mates. There were four males and three females, and the ones who left turned out to be Beauty (boy), Frisky (girl), Adrienne, namesake of Rosemary's Baby, and Sam, who joined a doctor and his wife on their cross-country honey-moon as they drove to their new home in San Francisco.

By week nine we were flooded with responses to our newspaper ad. We couldn't find any fault with the prospective new homes, but I believe we knew in our hearts that it was already too late—we had kept them for too long. Nonetheless, as I described the remaining kittens, an appropriate prospective owner seemed to perfectly match each one, but it was with reluctance that we drove the long-haired, tiger-striped male, who most closely resembled his mother, to a family in Dorchester who gave us no reason to believe that "Fuzz" would have anything but the best of care in a loving home. I had to hold back tears I said good-bye to him. Misery and guilt took over during the next couple of days, knowing I could not adjust to his being gone and feeling somewhat squeamish inside at the thought of what I was about to do.

I phoned these good folks, and promised them I'd replace "Fuzz" with the nicest kitten I could find if only I could have him back. Though I have rarely felt more foolish, they were not only gracious, but they were also sympathetic. A trip to the pet shop, two rides in a taxi, and I was on my way home with "Fuzz." The next thing to be dealt with was how to explain my impetuousness to my own family. Worse yet was unpromising "Spot" and "Little Gray" to the people waiting for them. I still cringe when I think of what agreeing to keep Fluffy in the first place had gotten me into. I needn't have worried about my family. They acted as relieved as I felt when they saw me getting out of the cab with "Fuzz." Later when given the news, the ones who were not about to get the other two were polite and understanding, albeit somewhat puzzled.

"Fuzz," "Spot," and "Little Gray" were merely identification tags for our own use while the kittens remained with us. They were never intended to be permanent names; only one of them stuck.

From the day "Fuzz" came back, it went unspoken that none of the three were going anywhere. Within seconds of his arrival, he became "Teddy," because, as his Nana noted, He looks just like a teddy bear." It took a while longer to come up with something suitable for the little gray, tiger-striped female. Since she could walk, this kitten would size up from head to toe anyone who came into her view, and she would either give her acceptance or scornfully disdain the recipient of her gaze. This ability put me on the defensive for many years to come, when feelings were genuinely hurt. "Your cat hates me. She is giving me a dirty look."

Yes, *she was. Sorry.*

She was also loving, naughty, and adorable, so a name was needed that suggested a cute baby with time-wizened adult eyes. "Little Gray" became "Mary Ann." More and more, the 'Ann" was dropped until, eventually, she was just "Mary."

"Spot," however, remained "Spot." All the brain-racking and suggestions didn't remove the prominent spot from his nose; and since it was frequently observed that he was "smart as a dog," there seemed no need for a change. Still, it was such a common, undistinguished name for an animal that was to grow as enormous and sleek as he did; and it was a bit of an embarrassment to introduce him as merely "Spot." Teddy loved everyone, Mary favored me, but from the beginning, Spot was no one's but mine.

We knew from early on that these kittens would bring changes into our lives, but it took a while to realize that a metamorphosis had taken place. No longer did kittens live with us; we lived in a circus.

Although Toodles and Fluffy were outdoor cats, as had been Penny, we had hoped to keep the little ones indoors. The long enclosed side and front porches were sufficient for them to get all the exercise and fresh air they needed and to give them their space. This arrangement lasted for about six months; but when summer was in full bloom, the sounds and scents drifting through the screens were an irresistible temptation, and the kittens became jumpers and leapers. One afternoon I just opened the front door to their delight and freedom.

This move was fine for them, but I was never to be without a certain cloud of fear hanging over my head that someday I might come down the street to find a mound of crushed fur, and regardless of what was right or wrong in the debate of freedom versus safety, I knew I would have taken the full blame for myself and likely have kept it for the rest of my life. Thankfully, I never had the experience. But we were not to be without tragedy, although it did not come until other cats in another time.

In our cottage, the kitchen jutted out from the main body of the house, as did the porches, so that on three sides were low-hanging roofs. "The babies" had access to these roofs from the bedroom windows as well as from front and side fences. Sunning themselves on any of the roofs was a favorite pastime, until one of us walked by the house, which would bring one or all of them, crying, to the edge. As soon as we were in reach, we could expect a flier minus a parachute to land on our backs, heads, or shoulders. Where were you in those days, *America's Favorite Home Videos?*

One spring morning when we all had left for the day someone made the mistake of leaving a bag filled with wool skeins of multi sizes and colors. How long did it take them? We will never know how much work and fun went into the disarray of our adjoining living-dining rooms. We left a normal house and returned to a carnival. Streams of color festooned every lampshade, table leg, chair leg, and doorknob in sight. Was it one or two of the others or was it he himself who wrapped up Ted like a gift? Definitely the right time for a friend to drop in and ask semi-sarcastically, "Who's your interior decorator?"

Go home.

I always rued the day one of the vets that we used told my mother the cats would thrive on canned vegetables. I call them "the Veg-All years," when Nana would faithfully open the cans and mash up about two tablespoons of vegetables on each cat's plate before adding a small amount of table meat or canned cat food. When this practice began, I counted on the cats hating the stuff, but my heart sank at the thought of the years of monumental feeding rituals ahead of us when all five dove into the mixture and licked their little chops with delight.

I eventually phased out the process when my mother's eyesight began failing and all cat chores fell my way. But during the Veg-All years, we produced not cats but humongous monsters weighing in from eighteen to twenty-five pounds each, that would cause passersby to stop and ogle over our fence, at times asking, 'Are they *really* cats?"

"Yes."

"What do you feed them?"

"The neighborhood children."

Nothing against anyone's kids; there simply weren't any around anymore. In fact, there was such a dearth of children, the school next to the dike, which Jeannine attended through sixth grade, was eventually torn down for lack of use. Anyway, it made for a good cat joke.

Mary and Fluffy grew fatter and fatter and except that Fluffy was fluffy and Mary was short-haired, their mannerisms were very similar. "The Footballs" they were called. One or the other of us always had a lap filled with either or both. Mary was affectionate and very close to us, but Fluffy was a twenty-four hour love machine, purring loudly and constantly, looking into our eyes with more adoration than any of us felt we had a right to receive. One dear little furry soul had so much love to give in her lifetime that, if it could have been bottled, I believe it would have been enough to share with every emotionally starved child in the world. Only one more cat was to be her equal, but Jo Jo did not come into our lives until years after Fluffy was gone.

Their overweight was always something of a worry in the back of my mind, but these cats were not overfed; their diet was as fat-free as we could make it, and they were as active as any house cats with an average lifestyle.

Mary did not like overnight company and was not in the least bit shy in letting it be known. If her dirty looks were not sufficient to convince one to shorten his or her visit, there were other tactics to resort to. If some unsuspecting soul happened to place any object at all on the headboard of their guest bed, the guest would not be long asleep before the item would be dropped on his or her head. One female cousin: "She threw this book on me. I'm not kidding you. Your cat actually threw a book at me." *I know.*

"She hates me."

She probably thinks you should quit smoking.

Thus the time we had a visitor who turned out to be most unwelcome, although the boys participated in the harassment, it was Mary whom I counted on to hasten the departure.

My father had not seen his sister in over fifty years, so it was with loving anticipation that we all looked forward to a warm reunion with Auntie. She was to fly from London into Boston and spend a few weeks with us, then proceed to Florida via New York for an extended stay with my sister. Visits by anyone from "the Other Side" were rare, especially family, and since the people in our home are hospitable, it was with a growing fond anticipation that we proceeded with all the usual and many extra preparations. May 31 was her announced arrival date.

Auntie did not like cats, so we reserved space for all five (at the time) to be boarded at the vet's for as long as need be. Auntie simply adored John F. Kennedy and anything and everything to do with his life and times. Calls were made, vacation days secured, and itineraries drawn up to be sure Auntie would miss nothing from the birthplace in Brookline to the Compound in Hyannis Port.

May 10th was the first day of our spring cleaning. It also coincided with Fluffy's date with the vet to be spayed. Rugs were up; curtains were down. There was little food in the house. My father had eaten early and retired shortly thereafter. On our way out the door for dinner in town, one of the rest of us took time to sweep up the kitty litter that had spilled from a torn bag on the way up the stairs. We had a pleasant evening; and when we arrived home around nine o'clock, there she was at the dining-room table.

"Surprise."

Surprise all right. There's nothing working people with hectic schedules enjoy more than a surprise from someone they're not expecting, especially when stores are closed, supplies are low, and the house looks stripped; when what *is* offered is declined with "I don't eat that at all."

She knew of the misery that I had gone through giving up cigarettes, so what was her gift to me? A carton of Players. "You only live once, dearie. Light up and enjoy yourself." She was also well-informed on the doctor's prohibition of my father's use of alcohol. His blood pressure was high enough to qualify for *Guinness' Book of World Records*. Her gift to him? A bottle of the finest Scotch.

The cats gathered around, curiosity piqued. Auntie did not do very well in disguising her chagrin.

"I suppose it *is* their house." *Yes, it is.*

Weighed in the balance, this was still a minor inconvenience. Stiff upper lip. Make the best of it. Be nice. One out her complaining.

To myself: *Do your thing, Mary.*

Out loud: *All of you be nice to Auntie. Show her how much you love her. She's come all the way across the ocean to see you.*

Upstairs, my mother's bedroom was the only one with a door that closed.

Do the decent thing. Offer Ma's bedroom. Accepted with feigned protest.

The next day was too havoc-filled to reiterate its tales of chaos. It featured Auntie's delicate nose turned up at my homemade shrimp salad, the ingredients for which I had gotten up at dawn to purchase at the fresh fish store down the street. "I come from an island and see all I want of fish. I never touch the stuff."

I was an hour late for work, and my boss was all sympathy: "You are paid to be here on time. Why didn't you let them shift for themselves?"

"For the same reason I didn't call in and tell you I was sick."

That night: "I wouldn't dream of taking Alma's bed again."

"Whatever you say, Auntie. You're welcome to one of the double beds."

To ourselves: *But if you think we are going to lock up the cats to keep them out of your way. . . .* Auntie readied herself for the night. So did the cats—on her dresser, in her suitcase, on her bed, hanging from her hemline.

"Don't be naughty, kitties. Are they bothering you, Auntie?"

5:00 A.M.: "If I leave here at six, will I get the 7:00 A.M. bus to New York?"

"I'm quite sure you will, Auntie. Would you like one of us to escort you to Boston? Shall we phone Mary so she will be expecting you, or are you planning to surprise her as well?"

I wonder if my sister has forgiven me yet.

Those were the days before the earlier inferences about global warming. Winters were brutally cold; and in a normal year, the bay froze solid from late December through February, usually without thawing.

To a much lesser degree, I am also a Bird Person. Most communities have their Bird Person as well as their Cat Woman (did you ever hear of a Cat Man?). In the Neck, I have the dubious distinction of being both. I was particularly fascinated with the hundreds of gulls that were such a vital ingredient in beach life. Back then, on occasion, I actually had time to sit on a rock and indulge in daydreaming as I watched them swoop down, crying out shrilly when a bit of food was spotted.

Brought up on the theory that someone would die if I wasted any food, I had, and still have the inability to throw away any leftovers, especially during those icy winters when it is so difficult for these birds to feed themselves. So, it was with regularity that I made treks onto the ice with bags of anything I could find for the gulls—fat trimmed from our meat, pan scrapings, extra bread. Bundled up like Nanook of the North, and slipping and sliding all the way, I was never without company. While the older cats preferred the comforts of home, Teddy, Spot, and Mary trotted along-side me for as long as their unprotected little paws could stand it, at which time they simultaneously climbed me like a tree trunk, with one each ending up clinging to my back, and both .shoulders. Here they stayed until we stepped off the ice back onto the snow when I would nudge them down, and the four of us would race for the warmth of the house.

Spot and I had a running scenario that lasted all winter, every winter. No matter how wet the weather or low the temperature, he would whine to go outdoors—for about five minutes at a time until his feet started to freeze and he would come to the door, scolding me accusingly as he held up the frozen paw. His mother's fault, of course. We had been in the Neck for three years. Toodles loyally remained my father's cat and slept with no one else. On a normal evening, shortly after dinner, Daddy would let the cat out the back door and then take a nap. He got up later to watch TV and brought him in, both of them retiring for the night together.

One evening, there was a slight change in routine. It was particularly cold out, and my father and Toodles both went to bed early, while my mother was still up. The cat was kneading his chest. "Come in and see this," he called to her. Those were the last words that he ever spoke.

My mother had a lifelong friend who had left New York for L.A. around the same time we sailed for Ireland Promises of "getting together some time" were repeated then and resurfaced approximately once a year until more than a few had gone by. I doubted my mother would make the trip to the coast by herself; and since we were well off the beaten track of Eleanor's family and friends back east, it did not seem likely that a visit would be made by her either.

The voice from the past seemed to come out of the blue.

"I'm at the airport. Will be staying for about three weeks. See you in a little while."

There are people like that. The difference between her and Auntie was that Eleanor was pleasant.

"Okay. See you then," I said as I scrambled to put together a hasty meal and make sure a guest room was prepared. I needn't have hurried. It was a while yet before the taxi deposited Eleanor and her three weeks' worth of baggage on Bay View Avenue, behind the cottage. I sat on the back steps in the late August sun, Fluffy stretched alongside me.

Even before greetings were exchanged, Eleanor stopped short. "I can't go in that door. Look what's on the step."

Her fear of cats bordered on phobic.

"I'm sorry, Eleanor. She lives here and there are five more cats inside. I promise that none of them will hurt you, but you really should have let us know you were coming." "I will go home right away."

I'm sure she would have done just so. She turned to signal for the taxi, but it had lost no time in leaving. "What will I do? I can't go in there."

By now my mother had emerged from the house. A small, soft-spoken, genteel woman, few were her match in the ability to convince someone that their fears were groundless. This was a tough case, but my mother won out; and with great trepidation, Eleanor entered what I'm sure must have seemed, to her, a den of lions. As the rest of us knew, the most she had to fear was overfriendliness, but that would come later. Except for Bunny, the most recent arrival, who bubbled over with affection toward strangers, the rest restrained themselves long enough for her to digest her sense of surroundings and get over the shock of finding herself in a genuine cat house, the last place that she would have knowingly chosen for a lengthy stay.

Eleanor was going to give us a special treat while she was here. She announced that she would be cooking for us every day. Her first concern was to locate Boston's North End, about an hour's trip from the Neck. There she would travel daily and bring back with her every crab, clam, lobster, and array of fresh vegetables that she could carry. The remainder of the day would be spent in concocting every possible type of preparation our supply of pots and pans could accommodate.

We feared bedlam once the cats were exposed to such an available supply of seafood, but we breathed a sigh of relief when they paid it no mind. The sea air they breathed every day had apparently desensitized their noses for gourmet specialties that surely would have excited inland cats.

Of even greater dread was the day when Eleanor made spaghetti from scratch—one by one, each hand-rolled strand. They were draped to dry from every available empty spot from which a strand could be suspended. Eleanor was not the kind of person who could be dissuaded from doing anything that she set her mind to. She knew nothing of what incites a cat into action, and it was not likely we would be able to convince her. While the rest of us had visions of the cats discovering the dangling spaghetti and deciding what fun it would be to bat, knock clown, and roll around in, Eleanor continued to patiently roll and drape. We recalled our friend's "interior decorator" remark after the fiasco with the yarn.

Maybe we were halfway hoping the cats would come to the rescue. Eating food that had been exposed to surfaces that may or may not have been freshly dusted was not the most appetizing prospect, but to refuse it after her hard work would have devastated our guest.

Cats, like children, can surprise you when you least expect it. By the time they were ready to come in for the day, we weren't really sure what we hoped would happen. One by one they paraded through. Who would be the first to discover the new toys and make a move on them? One, two. . . five, six. Spot yawned and jumped on an armchair in the living room. The rest looked around as they passed by, not even stopping to investigate as they dispersed elsewhere around the house. By then, the pots were boiling as we assured ourselves that a little dirt wouldn't hurt us. Eleanor was using my father's former bedroom. Bunny had been with us for three years, and now, for the only time in his life, my mother was without his company while the fickle little fellow lavished all of his attention on the lady from California. So much, that she wanted to bring him home with her, but it would never do for us to be without him.

You'll have to get your own cat, Eleanor.

Toodles was eleven years old when we lost him to kidney failure, an ailment not uncommon to male cats.

It was two years later, when we had had Fluffy for eleven years that I came home one night and my mother mentioned that she had noticed the cat had been lethargic since the day before. Better get her to the vet in the event of a serious problem. It was February 4, 1979, and thankfully the good doctor made room for us that evening. The news was not good. Fluffy had suffered a heart attack and because of her age and size, the prognosis was dim. He gave her a shot and sent her home with some pink pills that we were to give her for two days. If there was no improvement, we were to bring her back; we were given no false hope.

It was with anxiety that we tried to administer those pills, and Fluff made it very clear that there was no way she would accept them. We also had our dose of guilt because she seemed to be using up her last strength in rejecting them.

"Please, darling, take them for Mama. We don't want to lose you."

A silent "no."

We couldn't bear to tire her any further, so with an uneasy sense of not really knowing what to do, we let her be and took turns stroking her, showing and telling her, how much we loved her.

For the next twenty-four hours, there was no change in her condition, and our one or two feeble attempts to coax her to take the pills met with failure. A second day went by, and the downturn quickly came. She was unable to hold up her head or drink the water that we tried to spoon-feed her. It was close to 8:00 P.M. when the vet was due to close. We did not call for an appointment. We told him we were on our way.

"I will wait."

Jeannine drove while I held Fluffy in my arms, rocking her gently, talking to her. We know it would not have made a difference, but have you ever, just once, wished for a siren or a police escort because at that time the mission in your life seemed the most important that you would ever want to accomplish? And at that very time, hit every red light in your path?

Jeannine drove as fast as, or faster, than the law allowed as we stopped at red light number one, two, three, and four. At number five, I told her to slow down, take her time. Fluff let out one cry, shuddered, and lay still in my arms as her bladder relaxed and drained all over my coat. It was over, but we still hurried to get to the vet before he gave up on us and left. We both cried as we rushed up the steps into his office, my dear Fluffy already growing cold.

"Don't blame yourselves. She was an old machine, worn out, that's all. I'll take care of her" may sound abrupt and unfeeling on paper; but this was a kind man, and in his way, he succeeded in comforting us. What saddened me most of all was that this dear creature was not even capable of having known how much joy she and her little family had brought into our lives. We gave her so little; we were repaid a hundredfold.

We went straight home to tell my mother, "She is gone."

Déjà vu! I have lived this before. Nagging at me was where and when? A look at the calendar slammed home the answer. February 6, 1971, 7:30 P.M. James Patrick FitzGerald, my father—an old, worn-out machine— fatal heart attack— ambulance—bitter cold— snow and ice—rush—rush—too late. A half hour later to my mother who had waited at home, "He is gone."

The Ancient Mariner

If his long fur and clumsiness suggested a teddy bear, the green eyes and cat paws were those of a lion, two animals that are contradictory in nature. Ted's shape and movements were all bear. If a person, he would have been one of the folks who manage to bump into and drop everything in sight. He asked for little and was basically a contented cat. When hungry or wanting to go out, one long, loud MEE-OW was enough to get him the attention he requested. When angry on the rare occasions he wasn't able to have his way, one or all of us would get a dirty look; he would grumble, stalk off, and the matter would be dropped, unlike his brother, Spot, who would leave no stone unturned until he got his way.

Ted was the only of our cats to have anything of a temper; and when he was angry or frustrated, he let us know it with his grumbling, and even then, he was laughable. Now and then there is a scuffle between a couple of cats, but the only serious confrontation came between Ted and a four-legged peeping tom.

I thought of the strays who came to my mother's bedroom window as the roof visitors. They came and went and included a couple of yellow toms, one of which we called "Thomasina," after the popular movie of the time. Another was a male replica of our female tiger, who camped out on our roof for six weeks. "Mary Boy" we called him, and we fed him as well at our cats' mealtime. No one bothered him, and he showed no inclination to come inside. We followed his sudden disappearance with a neighborhood search and learned he had been on vacation from his home on the other side of the cove.

Many more cats were to come and go, and I do not know which unfortunate visitor it was who aroused Ted's anger. It was one of those steamy, impossible-to-sleep summer nights, but I must have been at least dozing because the noise at the back window jolted me. Wails, screams, and cuffs were exchanged; and just as I fully realized what was happening, Ted was through the screen, off the roof, and chasing the other cat down the street at top speed in the almost-daylight of a full moon. I followed in my nightgown, feet bare and oblivious to the hard pavement underneath. The offender must have escaped in time as I grabbed Ted's tail just as it was slipping under a hedge. He loudly let me know how displeased he was at my interference, but he did not try to squirm out of my arms all the way home. Moonlight capers.

He was not beautiful, nor even pretty, yet Ted's features had the royal dignity of a lion. He was also cute and seemed to possess the exact proportions of each to perfectly combine young and old, homely and gorgeous. Various nicknames came, stayed for a while, and were replaced when a new view of Ted surfaced. One was "Baby Man," which stuck for a while, given by my oldest and closest woman friend who could not believe an animal of his size and weight had the agility to fly through the air and land with such precision on one of our backs.

Another was bestowed by the family as we all watched TV one Sunday evening as Ted sat atop the set. It could have been the Ed Sullivan Show. As the girl wonder of show business, in the early days of her spectacular career appeared on the screen, we all cried in unison "Little Barbra." The resemblance was unmistakable, but no, we couldn't allow that to stick. We didn't want Ted to go through an identity crisis!

Easily satisfied animals, as well as children, are, unfortunately, those who tend to be pushed aside in favor of the squeaky wheels. Not that Ted was ever ignored or neglected; it just took us a while to notice that he was a fetcher.

As my mother aged, her deep-seated conviction that everything she misplaced was something stolen by her granddaughter intensified. I was aware that this form of mild paranoia is not unknown amongst some of the elderly. Surely they know better than to lose their precious possessions. There was no question that a prized item had been taken, and no question that it was the youngster who had taken it. Thankfully, Jeannine understood as I reassured her that no one else thought she taking Gram's things; and there was always an apology when the lost was found—one notable time when we answered her pained query, "Where are my glasses?"

"You are wearing them," nearly resulted in tears.

However, it grew serious when Gram's false teeth were missing and a minor uproar ensued as the house was turned nearly upside down in search of her plate. It was finally found under the dining-room table; poor Jeannine was given a severe tongue-lashing before I could come to her defense. More tears.

"It's not fair, Ma. I get blamed for things I'd never, ever do," Jeannine protested.

She was right. It was unfair and beginning to seriously get under my skin, leaving us wondering if it wasn't time to take the extreme step of seeking new living quarters for my mother.

Shortly thereafter, the puzzle was solved. One morning, we all happened to be in earshot of grumbling and rattling in the bathroom. "Everyone quiet."

We stopped, listened, and watched as, after a few more moments of shuffling, Ted emerged from the bathroom with Gram's false teeth in his mouth. We said nothing as they were deposited underneath the dining-room table. We never knew the attraction or satisfaction that he found in this, but it was a while before Jeannine was again accused of stealing.

More mysterious was the occasional appearance of seaweed in the yard. Living on top of a cliff overlooking the sea, it seemed logical that now and again a gull might fly over and drop a strand or two. Other than their perpetual hunger, we knew little about gulls. (Did they build nests? Where did they sleep?)

In time the seaweed increased, and we began to notice it was sort of neatly piled, almost orderly.

Where was Ted during these sunny summer days? We might have known, should have known. We stood at the front bedroom window one bright morning, drinking in the tranquility of the scene before us, never tiring of the ever-changing features of its quiet beauty. This day, skies were blue, roses bloomed, bees buzzed, and white sails glided past on the bay. A sharp cry followed by the familiar grumble reached our ears. There he was, The Ancient Mariner himself—Ted, his fuzzy little behind bobbing as he made his way over the fence, dragging a mouthful of seaweed. Carefully placing it on the pile, off he went again, down the cliff, only to return in about twenty minutes with another strand. The walk was long, the work was hard, and he had no help; but as soon as we realized what was going on, we saw that Ted went back and forth, back and forth, from early morning until sundown during every day of the fair-weather seasons.

For whatever reason, this was his treasure, his accomplishment, and we had no inclination to remove it. There were enough high winds during the night even in the summertime, to blow his work away; but Ted, our own little old man of the sea, was not discouraged.

Teddy was a few weeks short of his fourteenth birthday when we began to notice a decline.

"Kidney problems," said the vet. "Can't be cured. We can just prolong his life for a while." Ted would be a hard one to let go.

Selfishly, we allowed him to be hooked up to machines. On every one of the four nights he was in the ICU, we drove the fifteen miles to see him, and on each visit, it was loudly announced over the PA that Ted had visitors. His face lit up at the sight of us as he hobbled on a splint that held an IV into his right front leg "MEE-ow" as he pushed his face against the cage.

Have you ever been to the ICU of an animal hospital? If we had not seen for ourselves, we would not have believed the array of casts, splints, tubes, and machines that these poor creatures were tied up to. Sadly comical, as if from a cartoon strip, but well worth the effort and ingenuity if it meant the recovery of the animal. This healing was not to be in Ted's case, but we sent him there with open eyes; and if our having him with us for another month was the result, it was worth it and bought us time to adjust to the inevitable. He was in no pain, and his last days were spent showing us even more of the affection he had given us throughout his life. One early morning, we took him to "the place," said good-bye, and went directly to our respective jobs, our eyes filled with tears.

Bring It To Mama Concepts of the most beautiful movie stars have, I am sure, changed from decade to decade.

Lifestyles and even my own personal preferences aside, I believe if every moviegoer over the past sixty years were alive to vote, the winners would probably be Clark Gable and Elizabeth Taylor. More about Elizabeth later. My husband, at one time, was referred to by *Jet Magazine* as "The Clark Gable of Harlem." Bigger than life, muscular, majestic, magnificent, Spot was the Clark Gable of cats. Tiger-striped on top, downy white underneath, with a weight of twenty-five pounds, Spot measured nineteen inches from the top of his head to the base of his tail. His blazing emerald eyes could easily be imagined piercing the darkness of a jungle path.

Highly intelligent and energetic, there wasn't a form of badness that Spot didn't get into. I don't believe there was a drape or a curtain that wentunclimbed, or rod that wasn't used as a tightrope. Fortunately, the style of our cottage did not lend itself to chandeliers.

Despite his macho good looks, there was a kittenish quality that remained with Spot throughout his life. Attention loving, he would go to any length to get it and hold it. When she came up from Florida for our father's funeral, my sister received a startling surprise in the bathroom. Looking up, she saw what she at first thought was a "Bloody monkey" swinging by his armpits on the shower curtain rod.

As Spot grew older, he became closer and closer to me.

While the rest of the cats sometimes followed me on walks in and around the neighborhood and to the beach, Spot was always there. At first, when I would go in for a swim, he would come to the water's edge and cry. Before long, he began to come into the water with me. Flattered as I was, I had no confidence in his swimming or my life-saving abilities. I was sure the novelty would wear off; but when it didn't, I felt I had no choice but to lock him in the house when I knew I was going swimming. Guilt got to me before long as I heard him hollering when I walked out the front gate, crying like any little boy who had been left behind. Future trips to the beach were made via the back door, walking the long way around. It was one thing when I blew cigarette smoke out the bathroom window as a teenager, but a thirty-year-old woman sneaking a swim behind a cat's back?

Back in the seventies, the dead-end street on the sea side of the house was unpaved, and in heavy rainstorms, a mud hole the width of the street would form in front of our front door and would, at times, hold water to a depth of up to ten inches. One rainy morning, Spot was on the other side of the "lake" when he saw me at the front door. All he needed to hear was "Come to Mama" as he plunged in, up to his shoulders, coming straight through instead of walking around the puddle; and I didn't mind getting soaked and muddied when he leaped into my arms.

None of Fluffy's kittens were very willing to let me sleep, and their means of letting me know never changed. Ted would get on the headboard and jump right onto my middle, using me as a halfway jump-off stop on his way to the floor. Mary pushed back my eyelids and peered in as I'm sure you've seen "Garfield" do to Jon. Spot's method was to pluck and toss the bobby pins out of my pin-curled hair. It seemed he tried to be careful, or my scalp would have been scratched more deeply than it was.

Besides breezes from two bays and the open sea, living in the Neck has the advantage of only one road in and out. Crime was at a minimum and fear belonged in other neighborhoods. Ours was where it was still somewhat possible to sleep with unlocked doors and windows and where, if an intruder happened along once every five years or so, he did not loiter for long once the dogs sniffed him out and barked him off.

Whatever the season, we were all usually in bed well before midnight, cats included, each settled in his or her place on our beds. Normally, they would wake up around 5:30 A.M. and one of us would let them out for an early morning romp, and return for breakfast around 7:00 A.M., by which time we were all up.

On this particular dead-of-the-winter night, the world outside was a solid sheet of ice. Thankfully, the doors were locked. We had only been asleep for about an hour when Spot, sitting on the headboard of my bed, began to wail loudly, plaintively.

"What's wrong, Spot?"

This was his 5:30 A.M. appeal to go out and in the meantime, there was plenty of food, water, and kitty litter. When I stroked him, he purred contentedly; there was no sign of pain. No petting or coaxing quieted him down, and after a few minutes, calls to "make him shut up" came from other quarters of the house. Spot would not shut up, and a horror tale from my sister flashed into my mind. Years before, her in-laws in Florida had a golden cocker spaniel that habitually slept between them, on top of the covers. There had been a hurricane, and they were house-bound on the first floor of a motel cabin for a few days. Outside, the water was knee deep. Inside, on the third night, they awakened to Goldie wrestling in the bed.

"Lie down, Goldie. Be still, Goldie. We will have to put you on the floor, Goldie" were ignored as Goldie continued to thrash in the covers. A flip of the light switch showed they had been joined by a water moccasin. How it got in was not known. If I recall the story correctly, no one was hurt, but Goldie and her owners left the Sunshine State that very day, never to return.

I wasn't looking for a foreign critter in the bed, but obviously something unusual was going on. We kept the bedrooms fairly cold at night, and I didn't appreciate dragging out of the warm bed; but the moment my feet hit the cold floor, I knew this was what Spot wanted. He jumped from his perch and fairly flew down the stairs, me on his heels. Could I have forgotten to feed them? No, if that had been the case, they all would have been nagging at me.

I turned on the light in the kitchen in perfect time to startle whoever had nearly succeeded in breaking into our back door. I heard footsteps crunch across the ice-coated yard as the would-be thief retreated back onto the street. Between the commotion in my household, whose members had all fully awakened by now, and relief that we had not been either harmed or robbed, we did not bother to report it to the police and neglected to show consideration for our neighbors. The next morning, the lady who lived in our present house told us her back porch had been emptied of her kids' toys during the night.

Sorry, Chris. Too bad you didn't have a watch cat! With as much mischief as I've already described my cats getting into, I am not about to claim they were angels as far as birds were concerned. However, I can say in all honesty that any bird stalking, tormenting, or catching, if done at all, was out of my sight. No surprise "gifts" were ever brought to our feet or doorstep as in my childhood when my father's cat, Minnie, would bring carcasses of rodents as big as herself for the reward of his lavish praise.

As with just about everything, there was one exception, which, I believe, must be some kind of a record for twenty-five years' worth of twenty-seven cats.

It was a spring evening when I arrived home from work, tired to the point of not feeling good. You know those times, when all you want to do is get into something comfortable and put your feet up for a few precious minutes while you use your last bit of energy to sip a cup of tea or a whatever. You don't even want to listen to the six o'clock news, never mind deal with any commotion.

I had taken the first couple of steps in this ritual and was about to, dare I say, relax, when it started. It seemed as if every bird that flew in the heavens had descended on our back yard, screaming at the top of their voices. We were giving Alfred Hitchcock competition.

Actually, it was only a few blue jays, but their shrieks were shrill as they swept down, up and around, like stunt pilots. Where was Spot? I had seen him on the doorstep when I came in. Was he going after them? No— it took me a few moments to size up the situation. As he sneaked around the corner of the house, going as fast as he could, belly dragging the ground, I saw that they were after him, and a quick glimpse told me why. In his mouth was a baby jay, peeping pathetically as its family made frantic attempts to rescue it from the big cat.

Barefoot, in a thin robe, I hurried around the house after him, in time to see him carry his prey into the shallow crawl space under the side porch, impossible for me to get under, and only a few tantalizing inches away from my grasp. I was down on my stomach as I met Spot's stare. His eyes were neither frightened nor defiant, not even guilty.

He just looked at me. He had dropped the baby, who was still crying for its little life.

This situation would have to be handled very carefully. The adult birds were now seemingly after me, which was unnerving—more shades of a horror movie.

Of all the cats I've owned, Spot was the most talkative. Others have been noisier, but no matter what, Spot always had to have the last word, even if it was just a mutter. He was also implicitly obedient, even when his will and mine were at odds. The fate of the baby bird was in my hands, and I knew if I failed, it would probably make me physically sick as well as heartsick. Should I get a stick and try to maneuver it out? No, there wasn't time to find one; besides with a false move, I might push it farther away, or worse, give Spot the idea that this was a game. My small ray of hope was to take a chance on his rapport with me. Deep breath, a quick prayer, and, "Bring it to Mama. Let Mama see the birdie." A chirp from Spot acknowledged me, and what immediately followed will always be in my book of minor miracles.

Spot carefully picked up the bird in his mouth, crawled the few inches toward me, and deposited it in my cupped hands. There was not a drop of blood, or a tooth mark, or even limp wing or foot. A careful examination showed the little creature was completely unharmed. The only evidence of its mishap was its wildly beating heart and a bit of Spot's dribble.

I brought it into the house, carefully wiped its little body, brought it outside, and set it down on the other side of the house. Spot had come with us and gone about his business inside the house. Outside, the jays had dispersed, apparently having forgotten the incident once I had removed the baby from the scene. The baby, thankfully, was not a helpless infant, rather a very small, young bird, evidently newly capable of caring for itself. I sat next to it and watched as it hopped around for a few minutes, then gave it a silent goodbye as it spread its young wings and flew away.

It was in the cold and icy winter of '82 that we noticed a change in Spot. Year by year he had settled down, albeit more slowly than the rest, and turned from a once hyperactive youngster into a mature dream cat. There was something about his eyes that we could not quite identify. They had dulled and seemed a bit starry, but we attributed this to the aging process, which affects animals as well as people at somewhat different rates. His vision appeared to be as good as ever and his eyes never ran as did Mickey's, who came to us with poor eyesight and related problems. Actually, it was Mickey's infection that alerted us more fully to Spot's condition.

Yes, there are cat ophthalmologists, and we had to wait a few days for an appointment with the nearest and the best. We had plenty of good-natured teasing.

"Will he have to cover one eye and read his letters?" "What style glasses are you going to get him?" "Are you going to let him pick out his own?"

And so on. In the meantime, Spot had developed an ear infection that would not heal. Medically speaking, eyes-ears-nose-throat have been loosely clumped together, so why make two trips if the doctor could see them both?

By the time the day of our appointment arrived, Mick's eye had completely cleared up on its own, so it was only Spot that we brought into the office. When we originally phoned about Mick's eye, we had been told to consult the ophthalmologist. Now that we were there with just Spot and his ear infection, we were told that" . . . he ought to be seen by a doctor of internal medicine; however, since you've got him here, I will look at him."

Spot was any doctor's joy; and in the years to come, he was the pride of the veterinarian community. Fearless, unflinching, obedient, and cooperative, the combination of his genetic makeup and personality made a lasting impression on those who treated him.

On that night, the doctor asked if there was anything unusual about his behavior pattern. Yes, we had noticed that lately he had been sucking on the hand wash cloth hung up to dry in the bathroom. We had associated this with silliness rather than thirst, because there was never a lack of drinking water in full bowls throughout the house. In fact, one of us was always accidentally kicking into one and questioning the need for so many. The doctor did not dismiss this, though, and told us he wanted to hospitalize Spot and run some tests. The last van making the thirty-minute run to the hospital had already left. Not many are the doctors in a metropolitan area who would consider doing for a human or animal the kindness that Dr. John Blake next extended to us.

"It is a terrible night, and I do not like to think of you ladies driving such a long distance on bad roads. I will drive Spot to the hospital and register him myself, at no charge."

The next evening we heard the results. Spot was a diabetic and would need daily insulin injections for the rest of his life.

We were later to learn that, at that time, he was the cat longest-known to live with this disease, just short of five years.

Who was to give him the daily needles? No one, of course, but the one who could not even watch herself get a flu shot. The thought of it unnerved me; but as is so often true, we never know what we can do until put to the test. "Time for your needy" meant climbing up and stretching out on the cushion at the end of the sofa. Never once did he make it difficult for me; if anything, this daily procedure strengthened the warm bond between us.

Anywhere between once every six to eighteen months, Spot would become lethargic, which indicated a need for an adjustment in insulin dosage. Usually, I could determine this for myself by the reading on his S and A's. Occasionally, a trip to the doctor was needed for a reevaluation. At these times, Spot sat quietly in the car, either on my lap or on the seat between me and whoever was driving. He was much too sophisticated, as well as too large, for a pet carrier, or even a leash. In the waiting room, depending on the availability of space, he sat either next to me on a chair, on my lap, or, on the floor. When I walked over to the counter, to the ladies' room, or into the examining room, he was at my side step by step.

Whenever we went away as a family, Spot would stay in the hospital for care and monitoring. He became the delight of the veterinary staff, a cat celebrity. On his arrival, all the doctors would come to greet him for a moment, his overwhelming size alone creating a stir.

Spot held his own for another four years, continuing his role as prince of the house and yard. His appetite remained insatiable and his strength and energy high. This was not a sick cat; except for his needles, there was no telltale sign that he was anything but normal and healthy.

A few months before his sixteenth birthday, Spot began to deteriorate. It started with a more frequent need to change the amount of his medication. We kept corn syrup on hand for the brief diabetic comas that he was slipping into. The doctors believed that, in the end, it was not diabetes, just the old age that would have come to him anyway. Spot was losing weight as well as strength, yet as long as he was comfortable and in no apparent pain, we were not willing to hasten his leaving us.

The long section of the road of my life on which Spot had walked with me was coming to an end. He knew it, and he knew I knew it. Except during extremely hot summer nights when each cat found a window to catch whatever breath of air that came our way, Spot had always slept across the top of my pillow where it was easy to poke at my pin curls. As he weakened, we could see discomfort setting in; and it seemed that instead of disturbing us with his restlessness, he took to sleeping in the bathtub, on the first floor. I do not remember the day when I phoned to make the appointment to have him put to sleep, but it was for the following Wednesday. This experience was going to be the worst, since I had cared for him for so many years, and I needed a few days to condition myself to his loss.

I slept downstairs, only a room removed from the bathroom in case he needed me during the night. Tuesday night, I felt a light jump onto the sofa, along with the familiar purr. I knew why he was there.

"Thank you, Spot, for being my faithful friend for all these years."

Wretched as I felt, I did not want to shed tears in his presence. Somehow, it would not have been an appropriate tribute to his dignity. For a full hour as I lay in the darkness, Spot sat on my pillow, not pulling my hair, but ever-so-gently stroking my forehead. When his strength was finally used up, he quietly got down and returned to the tub for the rest of the night. He had said his good-byes to me, and we both knew tomorrow would be easier. As matter of factly as possible, the next evening at 8:00 P.M., the vet's last appointment for the day, we handed him over to Doctor Sarah Moran, who had treated him with as much love as expertise. Thankfully, it was a peaceful passing for all of us, another icy February night not to be forgotten.

Bring It To Mama

Concepts of the most beautiful movie stars have, I am sure, changed from decade to decade.

Lifestyles and even my own personal preferences aside, I believe if every moviegoer over the past sixty years were alive to vote, the winners would probably be Clark Gable and Elizabeth Taylor. More about Elizabeth later. My husband, at one time, was referred to by Jet Magazine as "The Clark Gable of Harlem." Bigger than life, muscular, majestic, magnificent, Spot was the Clark Gable of cats. Tiger- striped on top, downy white underneath, with a weight of twenty-five pounds, Spot measured nineteen inches from the top of his head to the base of his tail. His blazing emerald eyes could easily be imagined piercing the darkness of a jungle path.

Highly intelligent and energetic, there wasn't a form of badness that Spot didn't get into. I don't believe there was a drape or a curtain that went unclimbed, or rod that wasn't used as a tightrope. Fortunately, the style of our cottage did not lend itself to chandeliers.

Despite his macho good looks, there was a kittenish quality that remained with Spot throughout his life. Attention loving, he would go to any length to get it and hold it. When she came up from Florida for our father's funeral, my sister received a startling surprise in the bathroom. Looking up, she saw what she at first thought was a "Bloody monkey" swinging by his armpits on the shower curtain rod.

As Spot grew older, he became closer and closer to me.

While the rest of the cats sometimes followed me on walks in and around the neighborhood and to the beach, Spot was always there. At first, when I would go in for a swim, he would come to the water's edge and cry. Before long, he began to come into the water with me. Flattered as I was, I had no confidence in his swimming or my life-saving abilities. I was sure the novelty would wear off, but when it didn't, I felt I had no choice but to lock him in the house when I knew I was going swimming. Guilt got to me before long as I heard him hollering when I walked out the front gate, crying like any little boy who had been left behind. Future trips to the beach were made via the back door, walking the long way around. It was one thing when I blew cigarette smoke out the bathroom window as a teenager, but a thirty-year-old woman sneaking a swim behind a cat's back?

Back in the seventies, the dead-end street on the sea side of the house was unpaved, and in heavy rainstorms, a mud hole the width of the street would form in front of our front door and would, at times, hold water to a depth of up to ten inches. One rainy morning, Spot was on the other side of the "lake" when he saw me at the front door. All he needed to hear was "Come to Mama" as he plunged in, up to his shoulders, coming straight through instead of walking around the puddle; and I didn't mind getting soaked and muddied when he leaped into my arms.

None of Fluffy's kittens were very willing to let me sleep, and their means of letting me know never changed. Ted would get on the headboard and jump right onto my middle, using me as a halfway jump-off stop on his way to the floor. Mary pushed back my eyelids and peered in as I'm sure you've seen "Garfield" do to Jon. Spot's method was to pluck and toss the bobby pins out of my pin-curled hair. It seemed he tried to be careful, or my scalp would have been scratched more deeply than it was.

Besides breezes from two bays and the open sea, living in the Neck has the advantage of only one road in and out. Crime was at a minimum and fear belonged in other neighborhoods. Ours was where it was still somewhat possible to sleep with unlocked doors and windows and where, if an intruder happened along once every five years or so, he did not loiter for long once the dogs sniffed him out and barked him off.

Whatever the season, we were all usually in bed well before midnight, cats included, each settled in his or her place on our beds. Normally, they would wake up around 5:30 AM. and one of us would let them out for an early morning romp, and return for breakfast around 7:00 A.M., by which time we were all up.

On this particular dead-of-the-winter night, the world outside was a solid sheet of ice. Thankfully, the doors were locked. We had only been asleep for about an hour when Spot, sitting on the headboard of my bed, began to wail loudly, plaintively.

"What's wrong. Spot?"

This was his 5:30 AM. appeal to go out and in the meantime, there was plenty of food, water, and kitty litter. When I stroked him, he purred contentedly; there was no sign of pain. No petting or coaxing quieted him down, and after a few minutes, calls to "make him shut up" came from other quarters of the house. Spot would not shut up, and a horror tale from my sister flashed into my mind. Years before, her in-laws in Florida had a golden cocker spaniel that habitually slept between them, on top of the covers. There had been a hurricane, and they were house-bound on the first floor of a motel cabin for a few days.

Outside, the water was knee deep. Inside, on the third night, they awakened to Goldie wrestling in the bed.

"Lie down, Goldie. Be still, Goldie. We will have to put you on the floor, Goldie" were ignored as Goldie continued to thrash in the covers. A flip of the light switch showed they had been joined by a water moccasin. How it got in was not known. If I recall the story correctly, no one was hurt, but Goldie and her owners left the Sunshine State that very day, never to return.

I wasn't looking for a foreign critter in the bed, but obviously something unusual was going on. We kept the bedrooms fairly cold at night, and I didn't appreciate dragging out of the warm bed; but the moment my feet hit the cold floor, I knew this was what Spot wanted. He jumped from his perch and fairly flew down the stairs, me on his heels. Could I have forgotten to feed them? No, if that had been the case, they all would have been nagging at me.

I turned on the light in the kitchen in perfect time to startle whoever had nearly succeeded in breaking into our back door. I heard footsteps crunch across the ice-coated yard as the would-be thief retreated back onto the street. Between the commotion in my household, whose members had all fully awakened by now, and relief that we had not been either harmed or robbed, we did not bother to report it to the police and neglected to show consideration for our neighbors. The next morning, the lady who lived in our present house told us her back porch had been emptied of her kids' toys during the night.

Sorry, Chris. Too bad you didn't have a watch cat!

With as much mischief as I've already described my cats getting into, I am not about to claim they were angels as far as birds were concerned. However, I can say in all honesty that any bird stalking, tormenting, or catching, if done at all, was out of my sight. No surprise "gifts" were ever brought to our feet or doorstep as in my childhood when my father's cat Minnie, would bring carcasses of rodents as big as herself for the reward of his lavish praise.

As with just about everything, there was one exception, which, I believe, must be some kind of a record for twenty-five years' worth of twenty-seven cats.

It was a spring evening when I arrived home from work, tired to the point of not feeling good. You know those times, when all you want to do is get into something comfortable and put your feet up for a few precious minutes while you use your last bit of energy to sip a cup of tea or a whatever. You don't even want to listen to the six o'clock news, never mind deal with any commotion.

I had taken the first couple of steps in this ritual and was about to, dare I say, relax, when it started. It seemed as if every bird that flew in the heavens had descended on our back yard, screaming at the top of their voices. We were giving Alfred Hitchcock competition.

Actually, it was only a few blue jays, but their shrieks were shrill as they swept down, up and around, like stunt pilots. Where was Spot? I had seen him on the doorstep when I came in. Was he going after them? No—it took me a few moments to size up the situation. As he sneaked around the corner of the house, going as fast as he could, belly dragging the ground, I saw that they were after him, and a quick glimpse told me why. In his mouth was a baby jay, peeping pathetically as its family made frantic attempts to rescue it from the big cat.

Barefoot, in a thin robe, I hurried around the house after him, in time to see him carry his prey into the shallow crawl space under the side porch, impossible for me to get under, and only a few tantalizing inches away from my grasp. I was down on my stomach as I met Spot's stare. His eyes were neither frightened nor defiant, not even guilty.

He just looked at me. He had dropped the baby, who was still crying for its little life.

This situation would have to be handled very care- fully. The adult birds were now seemingly after me, which was unnerving more shades of a horror movie.

Of all the cats I've owned, Spot was the most talkative. Others have been noisier, but no matter what, Spot always had to have the last word, even if it was just a mutter. He was also implicitly obedient, even when his will and mine were at odds. The fate of the baby bird was in my hands, and I knew if I failed, it would probably make me physically sick as well as heartsick. Should I get a stick and try to maneuver it out? No, there wasn't time to find one; besides with a false move, I might push it farther away, or worse, give Spot the idea that this was a game. My small ray of hope was to take a chance on his rapport with me. Deep breath, a quick prayer, and, "Bring it to Mama. Let Mama see the birdie." A chirp from Spot acknowledged me, and what immediately followed will always be in my book of minor miracles.

Spot carefully picked up the bird in his mouth, crawled the few inches toward me, and deposited it in my cupped hands. There was not a drop of blood, or a tooth mark, or even limp wing or foot. A careful examination showed the little creature was completely unharmed. The only evidence of its mishap was its wildly beating heart and a bit of Spot's dribble.

I brought it into the house, carefully wiped its little body, brought it outside, and set it down on the other side of the house. Spot had come with us and gone about his business inside the house. Outside, the jays had dispersed, apparently having forgotten the incident once I had removed the baby from the scene. The baby, thankfully, was not a helpless infant, rather a very small, young bird, evidently newly capable of caring for itself. I sat next to it and watched as it hopped around for a few minutes, then gave it a silent good-bye as it spread its young wings and flew away.

It was in the cold and icy winter of '82 that we noticed a change in Spot. Year by year he had settled down, albeit more slowly than the rest, and turned from a once hyperactive youngster into a mature dream cat. There was something about his eyes that we could not quite identify. They had dulled and seemed a bit starry, but we attributed this to the aging process, which affects animals as well as people at somewhat different rates. His vision appeared to be as good as ever and his eyes never ran as did Mickey's, who came to us with poor eyesight and related problems. Actually, it was Mickey's infection that alerted us more fully to Spot's condition.

Yes, there are cat ophthalmologists, and we had to wait a few days for an appointment with the nearest and the best. We had plenty of good-natured teasing.

"Will he have to cover one eye and read his letters?" "What style glasses are you going to get him?" "Are you going to let him pick out his own?"

And so on. In the meantime, Spot had developed an ear infection that would not heal. Medically speaking, eyes-ears-nose-throat have been loosely clumped together, so why make two trips if the doctor could see them both?

By the time the day of our appointment arrived, Mick's eye had completely cleared up on its own, so it was only Spot that we brought into the office. When we originally phoned about Mick's eye, we had been told to consult the ophthalmologist. Now that we were there with just Spot and his ear infection, we were told that"... he ought to be seen by a doctor of internal medicine; however, since you've got him here, I will look at him."

Spot was any doctor's joy; and in the years to come, he was the pride of the veterinarian community. Fearless, unflinching, obedient, and cooperative, the combination of his genetic makeup and personality made a lasting impression on those who treated him.

On that night, the doctor asked if there was anything unusual about his behavior pattern. Yes, we had noticed that lately he had been sucking on the hand wash cloth hung up to dry in the bathroom. We had associated this with silliness rather than thirst, because there was never a lack of drinking water in full bowls throughout the house. In fact, one of us was always accidentally kicking into one and questioning the need for so many. The doctor did not dismiss this, though, and told us he wanted to hospitalize Spot and run some tests. The last van making the thirty-minute run to the hospital had already left. Not many are the doctors in a metropolitan area who would consider doing for a human or animal the kindness that Dr. John Blake next extended to us.

"It is a terrible night, and I do not like to think of you ladies driving such a long distance on bad roads. I will drive Spot to the hospital and register him myself, at no charge."

The next evening we heard the results. Spot was a diabetic and would need daily insulin injections for the rest of his life. We were later to learn that, at that time, he was the cat longest-known to live with this disease, just short of five years.

Who was to give him the daily needles? No one, of course, but the one who could not even watch herself get a flu shot. The thought of it unnerved me; but as is so often true, we never know what we can do until put to the test. "Time for your needy" meant climbing up and stretching out on the cushion at the end of the sofa. Never once did he make it difficult for me; if anything, this daily procedure strengthened the warm bond between us.

Anywhere between once every six to eighteen months, Spot would become lethargic, which indicated a need for an adjustment in insulin dosage. Usually, I could determine this for myself by the reading on his S and A's. Occasionally, a trip to the doctor was needed for a reevaluation. At these times, Spot sat quietly in the car, either on my lap or on the seat between me and whoever was driving. He was much too sophisticated, as well as too large, for a pet carrier, or even a leash. In the waiting room, depending on the availability of space, he sat either next to me on a chair, on my lap, or, on the floor. When I walked over to the counter, to the ladies' room, or into the examining room, he was at my side step by step.

Whenever we went away as a family, Spot would stay in the hospital for care and monitoring. He became the delight of the veterinary staff, a cat celebrity. On his arrival, all the doctors would come to greet him for a moment, his overwhelming size alone creating a stir.

Spot held his own for another four years, continuing his role as prince of the house and yard. His appetite remained insatiable and his strength and energy high. This was not a sick cat; except for his needles, there was no telltale sign that he was anything but normal and healthy.

A few months before his sixteenth birthday, Spot began to deteriorate. It started with a more frequent need to change the amount of his medication. We kept corn syrup on hand for the brief diabetic comas that he was slipping into. The doctors believed that, in the end, it was not diabetes, just the old age that would have come to him anyway. Spot was losing weight as well as strength, yet as long as he was comfortable and in no apparent pain, we were not willing to hasten his leaving us.

The long section of the road of my life on which Spot had walked with me was coming to an end. He knew it, and he knew I knew it. Except during extremely hot summer nights when each cat found a window to catch whatever breath of air that came our way, Spot had always slept across the top of my pillow where it was easy to poke at my pin curls. As he weakened, we could see discomfort setting in; and it seemed that instead of disturbing us with his restlessness, he took to sleeping in the bathtub, on the first floor. I do not remember the day when I phoned to make the appointment to have him put to sleep, but it was for the following Wednesday. This experience was going to be the worst, since I had cared for him for so many years, and I needed a few days to condition myself to his loss.

I slept downstairs, only a room removed from the bathroom in case he needed me during the night. Tuesday night, I felt a light jump onto the sofa, along with the familiar purr. I knew why he was there.

"Thank you, Spot, for being my faithful friend for all these years."

Wretched as I felt, I did not want to shed tears in his presence. Somehow, it would not have been an appropriate tribute to his dignity. For a full hour as I lay in the darkness, Spot sat on my pillow, not pulling my hair, but ever-so-gently stroking my forehead. When his strength was finally used up, he quietly got down and returned to the tub for the rest of the night. He had said his good-byes to me, and we both knew tomorrow would be easier. As matter of factly as possible, the next evening at 8:00 PM., the vet's last appointment for the day, we handed him over to Doctor Sarah Moran, who had treated him with as much love as expertise. Thankfully, it was a peaceful passing for all of us, another icy February night not to be forgotten.

You'll Always Be My Number One

Girl

We learned to keep our pocketbooks closed. Open, they was an invitation to a certain gray-striped, short-haired female tiger kitten to hop in, curl up, and take a nap. Even as she grew and her unconventional crib tightened around her plump little body, and later, when she hung out of each end, Mary did not willingly give up her choice of a place to sleep.

It is good that we do not believe in reincarnation. Otherwise we would have spent many unprofitable hours in a search to determine who Mary had been in a previous life. She and Goldie, who was to come years later, and who up until then were the only two cats to resemble each other, both had the piercing look in their eyes of an old lady who had seen and experienced much in life and would have much to tell if you should ask.

Except for those eyes, Mary was in every way a kitten. Though she went out with her brothers, she was not a roamer, and we never had to look for her any farther than the bulkhead, where she would lie in the sun and look at us through the kitchen window. Indoors, she was always stretched across or squeezed on one of our laps with Fluffy, her mother, especially on nights when winter's chill would penetrate the very walls of the cottage.

Those were the nights memories are made of. Unpretentious as it was, the house exuded warmth and welcome from the amber-colored glass laps and rose-colored walls of the living room, to the glistening cranberry wide-board floors that extended to the dining room. As our "family" grew, it seemed a cat was added to every available spot in the decor. No matter where we sat, we were joined by cats. And this was particularly so if someone took a nap on the sofa, when the sleeper would be covered as thoroughly as if by a quilt. This routine was especially true in bed, where all pretty well stayed in their selected places until morning.

During my hours at home, I was never one to sit or lie still for very long. My interests were divided between up and downstairs, and there were evenings when, I believe, I made the up and downward tread as many as forty times. Mary paid me no mind and would wait patiently on the sofa or wherever else I had been sitting. I will never know what the giveaway was; but she knew when I was ascending for the night and without fail, she was by my side.

My father died a few days before the kittens were a year old. Had we known then what we were to learn later, perhaps if we had paid more attention to the cats' strange behavior, his life might have been saved. His death, when it came, was sudden and swift. Except for a couple of nosebleeds, which had alerted us to his high blood pressure years earlier, we never knew him to have a sick day.

He was not what you could call a neat man, although when the occasion called for it, he could rival any Jim Dandy. But when it came to bodily cleanliness, he took sometimes as many as four showers a day. Never could he be accused of giving off any kind of offense. So it was baffling when, around the first of the year, we noticed that every time any of the cats passed him by, he or she would stop to sniff at any part of him that was not covered. No amount of calling or coaxing would sidetrack the sniffer, and it usually ended with one of us dragging away the offending cat.

This activity continued for a few weeks, right up until the day he died. It was not until a year or so afterward that the mystery was solved too late, when we read in a medical column that a human body gives off an odor of impending death, detectable only by animals.

When preparations were being made for his funeral, the familiar accusations were directed at Jeannine, only this time it was, "What did you do with your grandfather's socks?"

"What do you mean, Gram? I don't know anything about his socks."

"Well, he has at least a dozen pairs and there isn't a single sock to be found in his room."

I interceded before a full-blown argument ensued. "Just buy him a new pair. The rest will be found later. Socks are not a top priority right now."

"I don't know why we should have to buy new ones when he already has so many"

Her words trailed off as I reiterated that the subject was closed.

My sister flew up from Florida and left immediately after the services. When everyone else who was coming and going had come and gone, that afternoon we were home, about to unwind after the stressful few days, when we heard the first of Mary's cries. It was a sharp cry, of fear as well as pain. She began to run around as if lost, first in one direction, then another. She was looking for something, but what? Then the parade began as one pair of socks after another was carried in her mouth, each from a different hiding place throughout the house, all to be deposited in a mound in the middle of my father's bed. The way she treated them, it was obvious she thought they were her babies.

"Rachel weeping for her children . . . because they are no more."

For Mary, it was for the kittens that she would never have.

For Jeannine, it was absolution.

Snakes and I do not mix, a not uncommon mindset, and one to which I am sure many people can relate. My fear borders on terror and extends to the unreasonable; it includes snakes that are large or small, poisonous or "harmless," dead or alive, and has nothing to do with what one might possibly do to me. I do not even like to be in a room with a magazine or a book that has a picture of a snake in it. If, due to circumstances beyond my control, I were forced to live in an area where snakes were prevalent, as my sister does ("They run under my feet while I'm hanging up the wash"), professional therapy would be mandatory. This fear established, another fact presents itself: there is never any telling as to what extent temporary madness can carry us.

It was midsummer and though not unbearable, the heat was uncomfortable enough. Shiny, cranberry-red floors need maintenance, in the form of a good paint-followed-by-polyurethane job about once every year and a half. No one but I had the ambition for this task, which was drudgery at its worst; but it was one of those chores that, once done, brought enough satisfaction to make all the hard work worthwhile for months to come. At least that is what I told myself as the image of my tired messy self, smeared in cranberry looked back at me when the paint brushes could, at last, be put away.

I always waited to proceed until well into the night when all was cool and quiet. Litter boxes and dishes were redistributed; and cats were divided among the porches, the cellar, and Nana's bedroom, where they would stay until the floors dried, and then some. They all seemed to understand when it was necessary to quietly go along with I lie program. No one fretted about the situation, except my mother, who seemed not to be able to stand the inconvenience of disruption.

So it was on that night when I "did" the floors. On these occasions, my mother and I shared a bedroom. After surveying my accomplishment with pride and massaging limbs, it was 4:00 A.M. when I finally tiptoed up the stairs I lie tried to slip into bed without waking her or anyone else. *Failure.*

"Are you finished?" "Yes."

"Get into bed, then. Try to get some rest." *That's what I'm trying todo.*

"Scratch" from the inside of Nana's bedroom door.

Scratch, scratch. Quiet. "Meow." Scratch, again.

"That's Mary."

"I know."

Scratch, scratch again. "Meow" increased an octave. "She wants to come out."

"Ma, it's only because she hears us talking. If we keep still and go to sleep, she will too."

"She only wants to get in bed with you." "Well, she can't. Ma, where are you going?"

"To the bathroom. And I'm going to let her out. She'll go right to you."

"NO!"

"Too late. Mary was out. Mary was running—not to me, but straight for the stairs.

"Catch her!"

"I can't."

No, of course you can't. How many folks in their seventies can run down the stairs in the dark on two feet as fast as a sure-footed, four-legged animal?

By the time I turned on the light at the foot of the stairs, my worst fears were realized. The dining room came first, but she didn't stop there. In panic, she ended up at the far end of the living room, where wideeyed with fear, she could go no farther. And I wallowed through the wet paint, slipping, grabbing at the walls, falling, rolling, until at last I reached her.

Snatching her into my arms, I retreated into the kitchen, out the back door, across the yard; by the time I banged on my poor landlord's door, my tears had turned to hysteria. I had been too angry to speak to my mother, and in contrition she wisely made her way back to bed. This kind man asked few questions; and though I do not remember his words, his gestures of comfort and concern eventually calmed me down. There I was in my nightclothes, with a frightened, paint-covered cat, bothering an old man at four-thirty in the morning. By his reaction, you would think it was no more than a regular practice for him to be dragging out rags and turpentine, assisting me in cleaning up both Mary and myself.

"But I've also got red paint all over the kitchen floor and the woodwork. And there are footprints outside on the walk."

"Don't worry. I'll take care of it."

And he did, then and there. By the time the sun came up, there wasn't a hint that anything out of the ordinary had taken place, except for the floors themselves, of course. I knew what would be facing me again that night. Oh, well, why do a rotten job just once when you can do it twice?

The new day was hot before it began. I was too keyed up for sleep and knew if I did doze off for an hour or so, it would be that much harder to get up and go to work.

The particular branch of the bank where I was employed was in a somewhat remote area of the city, generally thought to be unsafe for lunchtime strolls. Management went beyond the call of duty in its attempt to keep us happy, and extended their efforts to include our entertainment. The complex was surrounded by manicured gardens and patios where those who wished could work on their tan in those prehole-in-the-ozone layer days. That day we were to have a special treat—a visit from the Zoo Mobile. Great. What's more fun than coming from one zoo at home and going to another at work?

I had held up pretty well during the morning, and it wasn't until lunchtime when I had a chance to relax that it all flooded over me—anger, frustration, exhaustion. I had heard what a severe hangover is supposed to be like—a headache, tight eyes, dizziness, a feeling of somehow having left my body Outside, the Zoo Mobile had arrived and set up its hands-on exhibits. The two young people were pretty well in control of the assortment of birds, monkeys, other small mammals, and reptiles. Nelson, the python, had slipped away into the grass, and a number of brave bankers joined in calling and chasing him. Not hearing differently, I presumed he was eventually recovered. On the concrete, Michael, the Zoo Mobile driver, along with his female assistant, were handling a who-knows-how long boa constrictor.

"Who would like to hold Gloria?"

If never again in my life, that day I was capable of anything. I heard my own voice responding, "I will!" No one who knows me will ever believe it. My only regret is that there was no photographer. I, yes, I allowed an enormous snake to crawl around my shoulders. I actually held her in my hands as she squirmed at my touch. She was not a very nice snake; and as her face met mine, she hissed and spat, her long skinny tongue flicking against my cheek.

"Be nice to the lady, Gloria. Don't spit. Kiss the lady."

Yes, kiss me Gloria. In the frame of mind I'm in, I might be just crazy enough to take you home.

Mary was about five years old when I developed a back pain that was so severe it nearly caused me to stop functioning. There had been no injury, and medical tests and exams came up negative. Since arthritis was not diagnosed, I was not given any prescription for pain medication and I lived on aspirin. I had to be helped out of bed and aided in dressing. I was nearly bent over and walked only with great difficulty. If not for a ride to work and the consideration of fellow employees, I believe that, in time, I would have been forced into retirement.

For the most part, I slept on my back and stayed in the same position all night. Mary was always somewhere on the bed and, like me, would generally stay in the same spot; and if I happened to put her in one place or another, she would not move. It happened inadvertently. Mary was at my left side; and when I rolled onto my right, she filled the hollow where my back had been. Purring and stretching, she pushed herself against me. When morning came, the pain in my back was only half of what it usually was. Over the next few nights, I positioned us both; and the days that followed brought a gradual but steady improvement until, in a few weeks, my pain was completely gone, never to return.

What doctors and pills were unable to do, Mary accomplished as my back brace.

One January day in 1981, when Mary was eleven years old, we noticed the swelling on the left side of her face. It was only slightly noticeable and appeared at first to be the result of a tiff with one of the other cats where someone perhaps played a little too roughly and had cuffed and bitten her. Or, we speculated, it could have been a bad tooth. It looked no better in a couple of days, so we made an evening appointment to have it checked out. For the only time in her life, Mary hid from me when I came home from work that evening. We knew she was in the house and had little trouble finding her under a living room chair. She didn't have much chance of escaping from us, once we found her hiding place, but her fear was disturbing, and I felt a small dart of apprehension.

Doctor Theresa Brim was Mary's primary-care veterinarian.

"It looks like an abscessed tooth, but I believe she should be treated in the hospital," Doctor Brim said.

I was at work when the call came in the morning. The name slips my mind, but I would know the male voice if I heard it again, now eleven years later.

"This is Doctor— Mary has cancer of the jaw. Because of her age and the expense, we do not recommend replacement surgery; besides, there is no guarantee it would be effective and would probably only be buying her a few months. We'd like you to come in tonight for consultation." Translated: we'd like you to come in and sign the papers giving permission to put her to sleep.

Actually, Doctor Brim gave us a third choice, which I've never regretted.

"You could take her home and keep her for a while.

You'll know when it's time."

"How long would you give her?" "A few weeks."

Mary gave no indication of being in pain. She was able to eat and drink and kept herself immaculate as always. She even continued to go out and spend her days as usual on the bulkhead, lapping up the winter sun. Except for the swelling, her condition could almost be forgotten—for a while.

The first telltale sign that the end was approaching was the appearance of a very fine red line that would outline a tiny section of her face in the swollen area. In two days or so, the encircled portion would turn black and the affected flesh would fall away, eventually leaving a gaping hole in the side of her face. Those were the nights when I would sit on the sofa, Mary at my side. Tears streamed freely as I stroked her for hours on end.

A new batch of kittens had arrived the year before; and one in particular, Bo Elizabeth, the beauty queen of cats, had taken a considerable portion of my time and attention, and my love. Despite reassurances from the beginning, Mary felt threatened, and I have sometimes wondered if her cancer had partially been the result of stress. Our only other cat to develop cancer was also' stressed—for other reasons. During Mary's final days with me, I made sure Princess Bo was kept occupied elsewhere.

I meant it then—and it still holds true—when I soothed Mary. "You're my number one girl. You'll always be my number one girl."

I know she believed me, because whatever else Mary felt, I had no doubt from the look on her face that she was at peace.

We had a system. Close by was a cloth and a bowl of warm water with a tiny amount of mild soap. Mary knew when her jaw would need to be cleaned. Her paw covering my hand, she would gently nuzzle her little mouth underneath my palm; this was her signal for me to wipe away the accumulated blood and cancerous tissue. This procedure took place once or twice in the course of the evening. Was it awful? Yes. Did I mind doing it? No.

It could not go on indefinitely. Spring came, and one mild evening when the days had grown visibly longer, I saw that the red line had extended around Mary's eye. In every other way, her life had continued as usual, and even her very last day was spent outdoors. However, we were not about to wait and see how much damage would result to her eye. We would take her the next night.

She went unquestioningly into Doctor Brim's arms. "I can't believe she's lasted this long. You've done a wonderful job," Doctor Brim said.

Earlier, I had dreaded coming home. However in the world would I handle it if she ran away from me this time?

I didn't have to worry. Mary was fine, sitting like a duchess on a dining-room chair. But stalking around and around the chair, eyes wide, hair standing on end, was Bo Elizabeth, who afterward refused to come near me for a whole week.

The Leash

The entire Fluffy affair had just been resolved with our landlord, along with our promise, well-intended, that there would be no more new cats at 20 Chapel Street. As soon as physically possible, neutering and spaying trips to the vet had been taken by all five feline inhabitants of the house, and this accomplishment was cause for a giant collective sigh of relief. . .

It was October of 1970 and life had fallen into as normal a routine as it's possible to have, adjustments having been made for two adult cats and three growing kittens. School had opened, the Indian summer days were warm, golden-delicious. All was well in our little world—or so we thought.

"There's a lost kitten down at the school, Mom. He's sleeping in the bushes. The kids are feeding him, but nobody knows where he belongs."

The school was on a circle, at the end of the bus line, a favorite dumping spot for dogs. What better place to dump a cat than at a school? This may or may not have been true. In all fairness, cats who appear to have been dropped off could be the victims of an accidental ride in the trunk of someone's car.

"Are you talking about a tiny kitten?" Further discussion ascertained it was a young cat—yes, one I, too, had seen at the bus stop. Knowledge brings responsibility, so it is said. I knew enough so that I could not ignore this cat's predicament.

"Please, Ma, can I bring him home?"

"No, I'll bring him myself." *You might get caught.*

As it was, his tail poking out from under my jacket nearly gave me away. That it was a "him" was already apparent, and by now the little fellow was on the edge of being gaunt. After days of eating scraps from school kids' sandwiches, he vacuumed up every morsel of food put in front of him.

"We'll take care of him for a couple of days and put an ad in the paper. If there's no response, he's going to the Gifford Home."

Need I say no one claimed this cat that looked like a cross between a rabbit and a clown. Underneath was the whitest, softest bunny like fur. We were later to discover his ability to leap into the air, as high as ten feet— up, around, twirl, and down—off again, up again. But for then, his demeanor was impeccable. His top half was black and gray-striped, and the green eyes of a different shade than Spot's, were as if heavily marked with black make-up.

Determined to stand by my decision, I made an appointment to bring him to the shelter that provided a permanent home for any un-adopted strays. At the time, we had no car; and to bring the cat to his destination on public transportation would begin with two bus rides, followed by a subway and a trolley. Friends readily available to take the time to transport a stray cat for us were few and far between; besides, we were trying to keep his presence as quiet as possible.

We felt deserving of a taxi for at least part of the trip, so we phoned ahead to have one waiting for us at the center of town. We made our way down Bay View Avenue, hoping to be inconspicuous, in time to see the bus speed by the end of the street, seven minutes early. By the time the next bus arrived at the taxi stand, no cabs were in sight.

"We are only a few minutes late. Can you get us another taxi?"

"No, lady. Besides, I don't know who you spoke to, but we don't go to Brighton."

This conversation took long enough for us to miss the next bus to Boston. Another bus would not be along for an hour. Add to that another hour's worth of train and trolley ride, and who knows how long the wait between connections. The home closed at 5:00 P.M. and would not open again until Monday morning. Defeated. To be honest with ourselves, we had already been hooked and should have saved ourselves the first bus ride. Retreating, as we neared the house, a group of kids trailed us.

"What's in the box?" "A snake."

End of curiosity. We now had six cats.

We called him "Bunny," and from Day One, there was no question that he was Nana's cat. His favorite pastime seemed to be stretching out on her chest and gazing contentedly into her eyes. She loved him dearly, but sometimes I think she privately considered him a pain in the neck— literally. Some pictures make an indelible print on the mind. One of mine is the high, three-quarter bed with the white headboard in her cozy yellow bedroom. Whether bundled under quilts when the wind howled around the chimney outside her window, or sleeping in as thin a gown as a person of her generation would consider respectable on the summer nights when the cooling sea air did not reach her room, early or late evening, Nana and her Bunny retired together. Their position never varied—she flat on her back, and he cuddled on her pillow on the right side of her head, his pink nose nestled into her white hair, his right paw encircled around her neck.

Though he was thin and hungry when we brought Him home , there was evidence that this had been a well-cared-for, possibly loved, cat, and in time there was further reason to believe he had either gotten lost or had run away from his original home. As time went on, it appeared less and less likely that he had been a throw-away. To begin with, his refined manners were in contrast to those of our cats, who felt free to park themselves just about any place but the table, which they all knew was off limits. Except for my mother's bed, he would not climb on any piece of furniture and would go only to the threshold of the kitchen door, but never over it. "He's a good example to them," observed his Nana; however, this was true only as it applied indoors.

For the first fall and winter we had him, Bunny seemed so happy to be with us and to have a home that he showed no interest whatever in going outdoors. This attitude changed in the spring when he was older and more confident. Besides, who could resist the delights that awaited him in the yard and in the tall grass behind the beach?

Bunny was a sweet cat, one we all grew to love very much in a short time. So it brought us consternation when we realized just what a worry and a problem his forays were to become. The moment his feet touched dirt or grass, he would leap and fly like a jackrabbit or better yet, a greyhound. His speed caused us to be questioned more than once by passersby, "What kind of an animal was that?" Speed also increased distance, and evidently disorientation.

Bunny did not seem to have the homing instinct of the rest, and it seemed that one of us would always have to go searching for him. We are not of the "Don't Worry, Cats Will Come Home When They're Ready Or Get Hungry Enough" school. Midnight often found at least one of us, sometimes all of us, walking the beach, rattling a box of his loved dry food, or roaming the neighborhood calling him in hushed tones, hoping no one would report us to the police for disturbing the peace.

We always found him, but in time, this routine took its toll on our rest and our nerves. The situation climaxed the day when Bunny climbed to the very top of a telephone pole on Chapel street, stretched himself out on the cross bar, and took a nap. We tried, but knew in advance that we would be refused help by the fire department and the telephone and electric companies. I was at work and knew that even if I were to try to convince my employer that a cat on a telephone pole was sufficient emergency to go home, there was nothing I could have done.

My mother was home alone with the dilemma, tied up in knots, afraid to look, too curious not to. It must have been during one of the afraid-to-look periods that Bunny solved the problem himself, because late in the afternoon she phoned me with the report, "I don't know how he got down. All I know is, he came to the front door just as nonchalantly as if telephone-pole sitting were a daily occurrence." Surviving another cliff-hanger, we knew this could not go on. For one thing, at my mother's age, any more frights like this would be flirting with a heart attack. There had to be another way; but the only solution appeared to be unlikely, if not impossible, given Bunny's untamed streak.

But, we had only the $3.98 price to risk and, amazingly, a leash turned out to be the answer. From his first excursion, harnessed up like a little pony, strolling with his Nana seemed so natural that an observer would have thought it had been rehearsed. Those were pleasant times and also gave my mother the incentive to walk a little farther than her usual route down to the store and back once or twice a day. Of course, they never walked alone. An old lady with a cat that looked like a rabbit, on a leash, followed PiedPiper style by five more enormous fur balls, was a memorable sight.

After his first time or two, it was Bunny who decided that they would go out; and whenever he was ready, he would fetch the harness and bring it to my mother, never to anyone else. After he was hooked up, if she didn't immediately ready herself for the walk, he would pick up the handle of the leash and escort himself to the door, where he patiently waited for her to put on her wrap.

This procedure continued for about five years. Although the exact spot changed from time to time, for the most part, we tried to keep the gear in one place. One day, out of the blue, the daily outings came to an abrupt end. The leash was gone. We made a search, which we believed at the time covered every inch of the house, including both reasonable and unreasonable places where it might be. Every trash bucket in the house was upturned and examined; no stone was left unturned, so we thought.

Bunny had matured and displayed evidence of responsible behavior in a number of ways. Did he hide the leash? I didn't think so, as the first few days he, too, seemed bewildered at its loss. What to do? He loved to go out, but due to his extraordinary size, we had difficulty the first time in finding a cat's harness large enough to go around him, and it was no easier now.

Unanimously, we agreed to give him another chance to go on his own.

"He's grown up now."

Oh, was he ever! This was early in the days of the over-use of the term a-t-t-i-t-u-d-e. If you can imagine the smirk, the swagger, the sheer arrogance of a fourteen-year-old boy being given the keys to a shiny new Jaguar with no restrictions attached, you have some idea of Bunny's reaction to his newly found freedom. Cocky and obnoxious are understatements, and it took a few months for the swelling of his ego to subside. But, our decision turned out to be sound. He gave us no more trouble. In fact, he rarely strayed more than a few feet beyond the front gate and seemed very contented to lounge around the yard.

Life continued.

When we moved into the cottage, we were fortunate that some spaces had seemed tailor-made for our furniture. One such place was where a huge, heavy sofa fitted between the door and the window along the inside wall of the porch that stretched across the front of the house. Comfortable and suiting its purpose as the best spot to catch a nap and an ocean breeze, we never saw any reason to move it. It was easy enough to reach the dust balls with a broom without any shifting. Why we did one day after Bunny had been going out on his own for four years is beyond my recall. Perhaps we saw something drop down behind it that couldn't be easily retrieved.

All I know is the lost was found, the by-this-time-forgotten leash. Forgotten by all of us except Bunny. It took him only a moment to pick it up in his mouth and deposit it in Nana's lap.

We lost Bunny in August of 1984, a few months after we lost Ted. There was no long-drawn-out sickness, no pain. He just gradually slipped away. We ended up "taking him down," as we had come to put it; and though we grieved for a few days, the happy, funny memories of our little clown helped us to quickly recover.

The Little Cop Of Chapel Street

After six cats had dropped into our lives in little more than two years, it was natural to become somewhat paranoid at the slightest evidence that anything on four feet was about to follow us, but eventually we stopped looking behind us. In the three full years from Bunny's arrival, we had not run into any more orphans. Home free at last, we became known as "the ones who have six cats."

October of 1973 dawned, and one crisp morning my mother called me to the kitchen window.

Balancing his way along the back fence was a gray-and-white kitten with an impudent face. "Leave him alone; he'll go back where he came from," in unison proved my mother and I were of the same mind. Jeannine was strangely silent, and to this day, twenty-one years later, she has never confirmed nor denied our suspicions that this was a cast-off from well-liked neighbors. I still believe something was being covered up. *Catgate.*

I went to work as usual, and my mother saw no more of the new cat for the remainder of the day. Three more mornings brought the same performance along the fence. By Friday, his tactics had changed. Instinct or some other cat must have advised him to "act more pitiful." A face pressed against the window, a twitching little nose were more than we could bear.

"It won't hurt to give him something to eat—outside, of course. After all, we can't let him starve. He might yet go back to where he came from." *Sure.*

We didn't let him into the house or fully into our hearts until we started to worry if he didn't show up for a meal on the back steps. By then, we were as relieved to see the familiar tough little face as if one of our own had been lost.

If he looked like a punk, he was also cute, somehow reminiscent of an "Our Gang" member. Have you ever heard that someone had "the map of Ireland on his face?" "Mickey Rooney" was a name waiting for a cat— this cat, and its only deviation was in the form of his well-earned nickname, "Mick the Knife." Mickey would lunge at even the meanest and largest dog who ventured into our yard.

Once an unknowing or daring dog crossed the invisible boundary, it became Mickey's prey. Innocent features became fierce as he reared up on his hind legs, front paws positioned like a boxer about to strike. Around the entrapped canine he would circle, the Poor scared wretch whimpering and cowering in fear. When there was finally a brief moment of escape, the dog would make a run for its life, Mick fast on its heels, giving the trespasser a rapid escort to the edge of the yard. There was not a dog of any size or breed that Mickey didn't challenge. It was confounding that they were so afraid of him, especially since most were capable of having him for lunch in a bite or two.

Mickey grew into an average-size cat, but compared to our monsters, he looked almost tiny and maintained a kittenish quality well into his sixteen years. Adding to the mystery of where he came from was his failure to develop any endowment. There had been no spraying, no yowling. When we figured him to be about nine months old and brought him in for his operation, the vet informed us that had already been neutered.

"Impossible. We've had him since he was a baby." He couldn't have been more than ten weeks old, a small ten weeks at that when he first walked our fence.

No reputable doctor would have neutered him before then back in those days. We failed to convince our vet, who believed we had taken him someplace else to be done and forgotten about it. He was more successful in making us question our sanity than we were in denying his insinuations.

From the time he came to live with us, Mickey squinted and seemed not to see very well. He must have had weak eyes from birth, because in later years he developed cataracts. Back then, we put to the test what we believed was an old wives' tale about carrots being good for the eyes. While the rest of the cats were getting a variety of vegetables, Mick's diet was built on mashed carrots. It took a few months, maybe even a couple of years, but in time his vision improved and eventually appeared to be normal.

Outside, Mickey made it his business to pace up and down Chapel Street—down and up, up and down, day into night, day by day, year by year. "Patrolling, that's what he's doing," said my mother. "Keeping drug dealers out of the neighborhood," said I. Jeannine was at the age of discovering new words, new terms, along with holding the belief that we adults knew nothing of modern lingo. "He's a narc" met with amazed disbelief.

"You don't know what a narc is."

No, of course not. I was only a mother.

Everyone knew Mickey, dubbed "the little cop of Chapel Street." He loved to visit Mrs. O'Brien, a neighbor lady from Ireland, my mother's age. If she didn't see him for a day or two, she made her way over to our front door.

"Where is Mickey today? Tell him his other nana was asking for him."

He loved her as well, and many times, unknown to them, we watched from the window as he wormed his way around her feet and into her affection.

Out most of the time, but never beyond the end of the street, Mick was not much of a lap cat. His energy was used up on his "beat." And when he came in, all he wanted to do was sleep. Small and slim, he could stretch himself into the most graceful contortions. I never looked at him sleeping without thinking of an otter, and it was easy to picture him gliding through a sparkling pond or sunning himself on a rock. This was also the only cat we had ever seen that said its prayers. When not draping the back of the sofa or an easy chair otter-style, he would be on "his" own upholstered straight-backed chair, belly and face down, paws extended straight ahead.

Mickey was always a healthy cat, and even the cataracts were not serious enough to alter his daily activities. At sixteen years old, it seemed he had never really grown up. Peter Pan. So, it was distressing that spring when he rather suddenly stopped eating. Never a cat to ask for much, he looked at me imploringly and I knew, of course, that something was wrong. We had reason to dread the trip to the vet. Unlike Spot who took his visits in stride, this was a stressful experience for Mickey, and he screamed in protest all the way.

It did not take long for the problem to be identified as gum disease.

"It is difficult to tell you what to do. His gums need to be scraped, but because of his age, he will probably be at risk if we put him under anesthesia. If we treat him without it, we are still taking a chance that he might hemorrhage. If we don't treat him, he will slowly starve to death. Of course we could put him to sleep right now."

Nice set of alternatives to have to choose from at a moment's notice. We opted for number two.

"Do it quickly, please."

His cries were shattering, but it took only moments to extricate a chunk of tartar the size of a marble from each side of his mouth. Bleeding was minimal, and a shot of penicillin thwarted infection. He was quiet on the way home, but in the days to follow, pills to aid the healing were spit out with all the defiance he could muster.

Surprisingly, he readily accepted the baby food force-fed down his throat with an eye-dropper. In a few days, his strength and appetite returned, but we felt he was susceptible to any germ that might be out there, so for the last few months of his life, he remained contentedly indoors.

It had to happen sooner or later. Mickey relapsed into a weakened state, but we all agreed that he was not going to be put through any more terror. He would go peacefully at home surrounded by our love. Eye-drop feeding began again, but as he declined, this procedure soon became useless. Loving to the very end, Mick left us on a hot summer morning shortly after sunrise, purring his little heart out, raising his head to my touch, his beautiful green eyes looking into mine one last time before he closed them for good. We buried him in the front garden facing Chapel street, where the image of its own little cop can be seen through the years by all those who remember.

Turnstyles

There had been no new cats for nearly three years. It was late spring 1976. Jeannine was sixteen years old, well past, I had thought, the age of bringing home strays. Since she was to be well into her twenties when she would come through the door with Idi, Tina, Fred, Tiffany, Yoda, and the Upstairs Girl, I long ago concluded that for as long as I am her mother and she is my child, if we should live to the ages of one hundred and eighty-two respectively, the time will never come when I no longer have to fear that all-too-familiar "Ma, there's this cat . . ."

In fact, it was only the winter before last when my husband listened in disbelief from his pillow as I emphatically told her over the phone: "No, I will not get out of bed right this minute and fly to Philadelphia to take care of the cat that you found on your job. Take it to the lady who cleans your house. She's already got a number of them."

Stick it on somebody else.

Later that year, when I saw Linda Young: "Do you know that your daughter brought me a cat at three o'clock in the morning . . . ?" Yes. *I told her to.*

Back in 1976 I could not have foreseen any of this. An excited switchboard operator at work didn't even try to ring me at my desk. She left her post and ran over to me.

"You'd better get right home. It sounds as if something terrible has happened. Your daughter called up; and she was crying so hard that I couldn't understand a word she was saying, then she hung up."

Better not waste any time. My boss would understand. An emergency.

Can happen to anyone.

All was quiet when I arrived, Jeannine nowhere to be seen, my mother calmly reading the paper.

"What's wrong?" I fairly shrieked.

"Nothing is wrong. Just go upstairs and look on my bed."

A homely, odd-looking, short-haired black-andwhite kitten greeted me with rolling eyes. When I later got the story from Jeannine, it was all finally pieced together. That day in the schoolyard, kids had gotten hold of this kitten, were tossing it to one another, some twirling it by its tail, all tormenting it. She wrestled it away from them, and to their jeers, ran for the bus to do the only thing she could do for it—bring it home to Mom. Anger, fear for the kitten's safety, wary of my reaction, by the time she was able to call me, she had worked herself into near hysteria. Understandable.

"Don't worry. It will be all right."

It did not take long to get attached to the little male who would become "Cuchi" as in "Cuchi Cuchi," although "Cuch" ended up sufficing. He grew firm and fat, and what he lacked in looks, he made up for in sweetness. His walk was awkward and uncoordinated, an Ichabod Crane of a cat. I never hear the lines from "My Funny Valentine" without thinking of Cuch. ". . . you make me smile with my heart . . . your looks are laughable, unphotograpable."

His little cry was pitiful, but he blended right in with the family, got along with everyone and was loved as much as any of the others. Our hearts were just as broken exactly six years later when we lost him to a persistent urinary tract infection, accompanied by a blockage.

If photographed, Cuch's claim to fame would have been a trick often attempted but never mastered by any of the others. He loved the little nuggets of food that come in packets, so much so, in fact, that this may have contributed to his demise, along with the possibility that he could have carried in his genes a proneness to the illness that developed around age five, and for which he was in and out of the hospital several times that year. I say "may have" contributed because we always used these treats sparingly, and there was never a sign that any of our other cats suffered any ill effects.

"As long as they eat their regular food, it will not hurt them from time to time," advice from the vet by which we abided.

They all loved and continue to love the stuff, but Cuch was obsessed. All he had to do was to spot the brown grocery bag in the middle of the kitchen floor. Cuch had a habit that was cute only because it was part of his strangeness. He could spend hours tearing paper into literally countless pieces. The bag containing the box containing the pouch was no exception. Bit by bit a hole was torn until he found the box, which, in turn, was alternately pushed and dragged into the living room. This operation could last anywhere from a quarter to a half an hour. Once positioned, he would go to work on the box, and when finally pried open, each pouch would be removed and strategically placed to finally form a circle. Only then would come the relatively easy task of tearing open the packet and rewarding himself for his hard work.

"Unbelievable."

"You should have the cat food company come and film it."

Yes, we had the vague thought of doing such "someday when we had time." But procrastination let time catch up with us because we did not expect Cuch to die.

It was the very same day. We had received the call at 5:00 A.M. We never went back to sleep, and by 9:00 A.M., we were at my mother's bedside to give her the news that we had lost our funny little man. She herself was in the hospital with congestive heart failure. Not an easy time for us.

It was now 1982 and counting from Fluffy's death to Jo Jo and her kittens' arrival, our cat population had grown to and pretty well stabilized at nine. For about twelve hours we were down to eight, but before the day was over, the magic number would be reached again.

There would be a new family member to welcome Nana when she came home.

Idi Amin. From the big eyes in the round face, I knew what the name of this huge, short-haired pure black cat would be before I heard his story. "His name is Mackie." *Wrong.*

"Kandy is flying to Germany tonight. She is getting married, and they will live there. Her boyfriend is in the army. Her cousin promised to take her cat, but she backed out this afternoon. Kandy has moved out of her apartment. There was no one else to take him. He's really a nice cat."

Aren't they all?

No question about it, Kandy was stuck; and she was not the kind of person who would deliberately create such a situation. So, he stays. The point is definitely reached where numbers no longer matter. Somewhere after the fourth, or is it the fifth . . . you stop counting; you learn to bite the bullet.

Our hearts warmed to this dear soul, if not for his gentle timidity and satiny coat, then surely from the background from which he came. Kandy had found him shivering with fear, alone and abandoned in the empty apartment into which she moved two years earlier.

As reprehensible as it is to leave any animal behind, how much worse was a case like this. Idi was declawed and utterly defenseless. Sadly, he was only too aware of his condition, and everything about his demeanor seemed to apologize.

"Don't worry, dear, you will be safe here. We won't let anything happen to you."

An easy promise to make, a hard one to fulfill. The boys were pretty indifferent and seemed to take Idi in their stride, but for Goldie and Bo, the old proverb that "the female of the species is more deadly than the male" held true. We knew from their first sight of him that great care would have to be taken. What amazed us what that Idi understood. He reminded me of a handicapped person who tries to put everyone around him at ease. Idi was not a martyr; he was simply a cat who accepted his condition and was happy despite his limitations, which had to include separation from the rest. He enjoyed his food; oh, how he enjoyed his food, and he seemed equally content on the warm windowsill of my mother's bedroom during the winter and the cool shelves of the cellar on hot summer days.

"Why don't you lock up those two little witches for a change?"

Yes, a good idea, but one I never got around to. Anyway, sooner or later all things change, and this situation would, too, in due time.

Idi brought us a lot of pleasure. He had the faintest little voice, and sometimes I wondered if his larynx had been altered as well. My husband taught him to respond, so that when asked his name, his reply would sound as if he were saying "It." He also did a little box-step routine that Dicey called "the Idi dance" when he saw it being done by people. When told he was named after a head of state, and we emphasized this was for appearance only, no one ever had to go beyond the first guess for correct identification.

Idi remained in strong, vigorous health for the rest of his life. Kandy had him for two years, we for ten, but since this was in the days before rabies became an issue, we never had any reason to take him to the vet, so no attempt was made to determine his actual age. The only time he ever left the house was when I carried him to the one that we bought next door, and the only time he left there was that day during the January thaw when we buried him in the side garden between the pink and the white rose bushes.

Jo Jo And Her Golden Treasures

Did you ever have something useless that you have held onto for an inordinate length of time, for no reason whatsoever? You go to throw it out, but somehow you pause in the fraction of a second that it would take to release it into the trash. Once more you hesitate, then slowly return it to its place. Compulsive behavior, likely, because you know that you will never have use for it again.

Such was the case with a name, address, and telephone number on a slip of paper in my already overstuffed writing box. Contained thereon was 'the identity of a woman whom I had been told was an "expert" in finding homes for kittens. Indeed, I did consult her back when Fluffy's kittens were born. But you can be very sure I would never put myself in such a position again. After ten years, my mind finally convinced my hand, and the information was destroyed—forever—as I finally tossed away the small bit of clutter.

A few days later, I was counting days, trying to figure if it went out with this or last week's trash. Last week's.

It was 1980. A friend was in distress. Jo Jo had been her beloved pet for eight years. Her son was diagnosed with asthma and various allergies, most significantly to cats. Jo Jo was the culprit. I was not asked to take her, because my friend knew my hands were already more than full.

"Besides, she's pregnant, and she doesn't get along with other cats."

"That's all right. We'll manage."

I knew and liked Jo Jo well enough not to allow her to go to the pound, and none of us knew who would want a cat of her age with kittens on the way. To outsiders such as myself, she was reasonably friendly. To other cats, she was most definitely hostile. Now to figure out how to deal with Jo Jo, who hated everybody. Later, the addition of Idi whom everybody hated, would complicate matters even further. As our collection grew, we were to become more and more thankful for porches and basements; and we were able to work out a shuffling system which though took time and effort, at least was workable.

As street-wise and self-sufficient as Jo Jo was, I did not expect her to deposit her babies on top of me, and I was quite sure she would ignore any boxes or beds offered for her confinement.

There was no way to foresee that, of them all, she would turn out to be the one who, in old age, clung to me literally, almost fiercely, as if for her life. If only I had been able to live up to her trust. For then, she gave no indication when the impending birth was about to take place. She usually made herself scarce around the house anyway. So, one cold evening in March, shortly after 6:00 PM. when I happened to glance into my father's old downstairs bedroom, Her Highness was proudly stretched out; and nestled at her side, nursing contentedly, were three balls of slightly differing shades of gold. My first reaction was of surprise accompanied by a small thrill, quickly followed by relief that there were only three of them. After Fluffy's seven, ten years earlier, I was sure that Murphy's Law would again apply.

These were the first yellow cats that we had since my mother's Tommy, already ten years old when I was born. Jo Jo was predominantly black with sparse splotches of orange, so we did not expect any of her kittens to be a solid color. Red-yellow-orange--whatever most aptly describes them, this was my mother's favorite, so we knew at least one would be staying, and that one because "Goldie," a short-haired female, was as sweet and loving as any cat I've ever known.

From the time she was able to stand up, her little personality began to develop. It was easy to call to mind what little girls are made of. Even as a tiny kitten, Goldie was a "good" cat, mature beyond her years, never tearing around like the others. The staircase was hidden behind the dining-room wall. We rarely lit the stairwell light, so the upper area was usually in darkness. We soon caught on from the little cries at the top that Goldie was afraid of the dark, and one or the other of us would gladly make the ascent to carry her down. Her sweetness could make even the staunchest cat-hater melt; we never knew anyone who didn't love Goldie.

Of the two remaining kittens, both males, one was short-haired and turned out to be "Rusty" We learned from his new family on the other side of Boston Harbor that his favorite "cradle" was in the pocket of his adopted "mother's" housecoat.

The "bad" one of the lot was one that I would have named "Bobby." Long-haired and fluffy, he was to "snips and snails and puppy-dog's tails" what Goldie was to sugar and spice.

Neighbors down the street had recently lost their Rusty to a sudden infection during a routine procedure at the vet's. Our kitten came along just in time to heal the hearts of their three little girls. "Chestnut" grew to be enormous and beautiful, and we rested with the assurance that he was well loved and cared for. He was ten weeks old when he left our house. He was an outdoor cat, and on the rare occasions when we spotted him, he gave no indication of recognizing any of us, but, speaking for myself, there was always a tiny twinge of wishing that we had kept him. It took a number of years, but one day my wish was to be fulfilled, most unexpectedly.

Chessie was four years old when his owners bought a new home a mile and a half and a few twists and turns away from Chapel Street. None of us doubted that Ches would be happy in his new surroundings. There was an open field behind the house and across the street in front, a glade that contained every distraction imaginable to entertain a curious cat.

They moved in April, and a few weeks later, I ran into the man.

"I'm very sorry to tell you this, but Ches is gone. We are all heartbroken."

"Gone?" *Had he been hit?*

"Yes, he just disappeared. He was miserable in the new house. He would climb a tree across the street and howl and refuse to come down. The girls thought they saw him in a lady's house, but she insisted the cat was her own. I'm so sorry."

So was I—for all of us. The only consolation was that the people in our community were good and kind. In all our years here, we have seen many animals being treated well, only a few not cared for as well as they could have been, but never any abused. Hopefully, someone would be good to Ches.

When we kept Goldie, it was also decided that she and any kitten the future might bring would be kept indoors. Life was getting more complex, all of us were getting older, and none of us had the inclination to further monitor who was where. There was no problem thus far, as Goldie never showed any desire to go out; in fact, she rarely went near the door. So, it startled me when one night in late August that I saw her yellow face peering in the kitchen window out of the darkness of the back yard. "How in the world did Goldie get out?"

I carefully edged out the door to grab her before she became frightened and ran into the street. It was Ches, crying his heart out, dirty and bedraggled, who flew inside ahead of me. Ches had returned to his original home, the one he had never even visited since leaving as a baby—to us, whom he never had shown any sign of knowing when he saw us on the street.

Matted, flea-infested, full of cuts and nicks, he was nearly wild. I don't remember if we fed him or phoned his relieved owners first, but both were done in haste. The children were nearly inside out with joy as they drove over to pick him up. I can't think of any more heartwarming experience for an animal lover than their reunion with a lost pet. They were happy to have him back; we were happy to have had a part in it. Everyone was happy, that is, except Ches. The call came a few days later.

"Ches will not eat. He does nothing but cry. It is hurting us to see him like this. He wants to go home to his old neighborhood. Would you consider taking him?"

"Bring him."

It must have been the result of the four months that he spent shifting for himself. Ches was a mental, emotional, and physical wreck. I'm sure it would be the same for anyone or thing who find themselves outside of their normal surroundings in an environment that, even if not dangerous, nonetheless presented a challenge to their survival. It look at least the length of time that he lived in the streets for him to calm down and get used to a house again. It was another sofa, in another part of the room than the one on which I sat with Mary during her ordeal that I sat with Ches, giving him my own brand of psychotherapy.

First, there was the defleaing, which seemed an endless, hopeless task that brought back sickening memories. No flea deterrents in those days either. Mostly, I just stroked him, and talked, and talked— about anything and everything. It didn't matter what. Nor was it important whether or not it made any sense. All that counted was the love he was feeling, and, in time, responding to. The wounds healed, his scrawny frame became full-bodied, the dull coat again turned to silk. As soon as he was in fit condition, we took him for his neutering, which, for reasons known only to them, his owners had chosen not to do. Neurotic he would always be, but as for appearance, Ches could compete with any show cat. It is possible that in his wanderings there may have been some minor head injury. His behavior remained off-center enough to warrant the label "Ches the Mess."

I have never quite understood those who bring a cat home, when they either do not know the policy or attitude of their landlord, or else they know full well that pets are prohibited and they take their chances anyway. On an otherwise uneventful end-of-the-workday in October 1984, Jeannine came in the door with a Morris like, young, reddish-orange tom, his poppy eyes peering out at me from under her elbow.

"Where did he come from?"

"A girl at work. Her landlord found out she had him and said he had to go." "What's his name?" "Stripes." *Ugh.*

"Okay. Put him down."

I told Jeannine that he could stay but that the name had to go. He was, and still is, an odd little guy in the ways he related to us; but on his own, he is a typical bad little boy.

When I was a child, the family knew a man who was the same age as my parents, but who was so youthful looking and fun-loving that for many years I believed he also was a child, just a little bigger than the rest of us. I didn't realize it at the time, but this gentleman was one of the most intelligent persons to ever grace the planet. I saw only another kid. Hesitant as I was to offend a distinguished intellectual, there still could be no other name for the newest cat but "Fred."

Fred loved to feign independence, and there is no way for him to scoot away faster than when I make a grab for him and catch him for a moment before he squirms away, half-singing to him, "I'm gonna hug you. I'm gonna kiss you. I'm gonna squeeze you. 'Cause I love you." As soon as he's gone, I pretend I couldn't care less, and after ignoring him for a few moments, peek out of the corner of my eye and find him on his back, two front paws pressed together, prayer like, rolling from side to side, opening and closing his eyes to see if I'm watching. As soon as I make a move toward him, the game starts again. "Silly" my husband calls him.

In the cottage, there was a door leading into the cellar from the dining room. This was a heavily walkedon area, and I always kept a small throw rug in place there. As in many beach houses, there was a space of about half an inch between the door and the threshold, enabling Fred to go through the door, reach back under, and get hold of the rug with his paw. In time, he found he could pull the entire rug under the door and make a bed for himself on it in the darkness and privacy at the top of the cellar stairs.

My husband used to maintain that cats do not understand a single word spoken to them, even declaring they don't recognize their names.

Our life and work situation necessitated a commuter marriage, and most of Dicey's week was spent in New Bedford, fifty-five miles to the south of the Neck. While home, he did his best to ignore the cats' activities as much as possible. Here was my chance for some fun.

"Dicey, I'll prove to you that not only do cats understand every word you say, they are also able to follow instructions to the letter."

All I had to do was pick Fred up, hold him still, look him in the eye, and tell him what to do with the rug.

"Do you understand, Fred, exactly what I want you to do?"

This was easy. I opened the cellar door and put Fred inside; he immediately complied. The look on Dicey's face combined amazement, disgust, belief, and disbelief. The deceit was our little secret, mine and Fred's, and it's only now that I confess, to Dicey, that it was all a setup! In any case, he never again accused cats of not understanding what was said to them. And we are thankful that he never asked for any more proof, either.

Shortly after her kittens were born, Jo Jo, too, took her trip to the vet, and as in all such cases, she became fuller, calmer, and friendlier. For the most part, she was not happy unless she was outdoors. That had been her background before she came to us, and we saw no reason to change it. She took over where Mary left off, sunning herself on the bulkhead, winter or summer. We could always see her from the kitchen and, like Mary, she never strayed off. Only as she aged did an occasional pinprick of worry fleetingly cross my mind, quickly dismissed.

Indoors, she had become a clinging vine to the point where I could barely move and never sit down without her demanding to be held. I couldn't resist her, and many have been the times when I would give all my possessions to have her under my feet again, where I knew she was safe.

She was fifteen years old on that horrifyingly unforgettable weekend that I had so unknowingly looked forward to.

I have never cut my ties to New York. If the Neck is Never Never Land, New York is reality, the mainstream. My instructions are that no matter where I am at death, my ashes are to be returned there. A doctor's visit always provided a handy excuse for a trip home. This time, it was to be followed by a couple of days visiting with relatives at what used to be the family's farm in New Jersey, now twelve acres of mostly woods and fields, only a small vegetable garden left of the seemingly endless rows of crops remembered from my childhood.

Ahh, what a luxury to one who has always been the caregiver, for someone else to do the cooking and serving and other small forms of pampering, even if just for a short time.

Looking back, however, the weekend did not start out well. At home, I had to forcibly extract Jo Jo from my arms and in a slightly grudging way felt she was the reason I had missed the local train into Boston and had to wait nearly half an hour for the next. It wasn't the penetrating March cold that I minded so much as the anxiety of whether or not I'd make the New York train out of South Station. I needn't have worried, there was even a little time to spare—enough time to turn around and go home, which I later unreasonably blamed myself for not doing.

In the meantime, the sun was fully up, my mood brightening along with the day, and I gradually relaxed and enjoyed myself as I had set out to do. The doctor's visit behind me, the bus ride to Jersey was its usual delight. It never ceased to amaze me how vastly different are the change of seasons in areas separated by only a couple of hundred miles or so. New spring greens dotted the landscape as we rolled into the country. I had left patches of ice back in Massachusetts.

I welcomed my cousin's invitation to take a nap and fell into a sleep so deep that I was weak with exhaustion on awakening, taking nearly an hour to summon the strength to get up and show some sort of response to their hospitality. I had been in the throes of a dream—an awful, terrifying dream in which an angry woman with red hair and thick glasses, the proprietor of a cat shelter, confronted me.

"They bring them here and leave them, and look at what happens to them," she screamed as her hand waved me to the scene of a street strewn with cats— all of them dead. In the next scene, I was home. The cats were gone—all of them. I called and I called. Nothing. I screamed and woke up, oh, so grateful to see daylight around me and to know none of it had really happened. I knew I should not have eaten so much before lying down.

We reminisced at a leisurely dinner, no cats to feed or clean up after, though I accompanied my cousin up and down the stairs as she tended to hers.

I decided to get an early start the next morning and have a relaxing evening at home rather than arrive late and have to scramble to get ready for work the next morning. Downstairs, two of their cats perched atop a chest of drawers. When I passed by on the way to the door, one of them reached out for me; and as I stopped to give it a bit of attention, they both began to poke at me, intently, persistently, looking me in the face as if urgently trying to tell me something. These cats did not know me, and the most interest they ever expressed was a cross between half-hearted friendliness and mild curiosity. I observed offhandedly to my cousin, somewhat amused, "They want to speak to me." Somehow it was unnerving, but I proceeded with my good-byes and made my way back to the city.

It was Sunday morning and New York was in magnificent bloom. Vendors' daffodils, tulips, and lilies seemed to occupy every corner. I took the long way to Penn Station. My train was not due to leave for another hour, a good chance to enjoy the warm sunshine as well as the bustling sidewalks that I missed so much. The sun was hot, and I ended up carrying the heavy tweed coat in which I had left Boston.

The delightful features of the day later diminished— gradually, but I was to remember them for their dramatic contrast _ with what I was to find back in Massachusetts.

The train's departure was delayed by an hour, for reasons muffled when announced over 'the PA. The station was packed. Somehow I had expected it to be empty, figuring that those planning to be "home for Easter" would have traveled the day before. The only seat available was in a smoking car, and for reasons also unknown, the trip that normally kept to its five-hour duration stretched into seven hours. Behind me was a woman with three young children, all squeezed into two seats.

I'm sure it wouldn't have made any difference if there had been sufficient seats, because the kids ran a screaming marathon up and down the aisle from the moment we pulled out of New York until two or three minutes before we arrived in Boston. The conductor made his presence scarce, and the only attempt at control from the mother came in the form of a bland hourly admonition to "be nice, or Mother won't be pleased."

By the time I entered the station for my local train, I was exhausted, with pounding head and frayed nerves. On the final leg of my trip, the local bus took the long way home because it was Sunday and two routes were combined. Walking from the stop, I shuddered. The wind did not stop at being bone-chilling; it tore into the very soul. Above, the trees were stark and bare, the sky starless and bleak. The entire atmosphere seemed enshrouded in evil. The cottage is only a few feet away.

Hurry, hurry, get inside. Collapse. Warm up.

I quickened my pace as if seeking refuge.

As I opened the door, I was greeted by Mickey, Little Kitty, and Ches.

Let them out for a little while. Likely they've been in all day.

No one was home, and I guessed they weren't expecting me until later.

Fine. I've got the house to myself—for once.

I didn't see Jo Jo. She would have been in my lap by now. Someone probably let her out earlier. She couldn't be far and would come in with the rest. Not more than ten minutes passed. I had barely removed my coat when I heard the dogs barking—frantically, angrily, wildly. In moments I was at the door, and in flew the trio I had let out. Where was Jo Jo? I stepped outside, calling, calling. The neighbor on the other side of the fence heard me.

"A pack of dogs came through and killed a cat about half an hour ago. I just heard them bark and came out to see if they've got another one." Panic gripped at my heart.

"What did the cat look like?"

"It was gray. I don't think it was one of yours." Relief. Sorrow—for whoever it was. Jo Jo must be hiding, either someplace out here or in the house. My search picked up speed—outside, inside, out again. Across the street, bordering the back yard, the lady who lived there called to me from her front door.

"Are you looking for your cat? I'm so sorry. She was the one. First they killed her, then they dragged her away. I tried to fend them off with a shovel, but there were three of them. I didn't have a chance."

Mrs. Dunn had been mistaken. The streetlights had evidently changed the color of the cat that she had seen.

"Thank you, Helen. There is no way I can put into words what I am feeling right now."

I slowly returned to the house—calm, tearless, numb with grief—and guilt. Oddly, my cousin had tried to convince me to accept a $10 bill.

"My treat. Take a taxi from the train. Why wait around for the bus?"

Why, indeed? But, true to my own nature, I refused. I am not comfortable taking money or anything else if it hasn't been "earned" or is not justified by some very special reason or occasion. Ten dollars would have bought me ten minutes—the difference between Jo Jo's life and death. Could I have saved her if I had been there? Who, in such a circumstance ever knows? But anyone who has been there is painfully familiar with the lasting torment of those two little words, "what if?"

Life did not easily return to normal. The *joi de vivre* has never fully returned to me. A torn heart can heal only so far; it will forever remain tender to the touch. I dreamed of the dogs for weeks. And always, they were crashing through the windows, snarling, teeth bared, reared to tear us all apart, before I awakened in a sweat, heart pounding in terror—the terror that Jo Jo must have felt. It would be years before our secure little sanctuary would feel safe again.

One fact remained certain. My cats would never roam outdoors again, not until the rule of the Kingdom of God brings peace to the animal world as well as the world of mankind, in fulfillment of His promise at Isaiah chapter 11, verses 6 through 9:

And the wolf will actually reside for a while with the male lamb, and with the kid the leopard itself will lie down, and the calf and the maned young lion and the well-fed animal all together, and a mere little boy willbe leader over them.

And the cow and the bear themselves will feed; together their young ones will lie down. And even the lion will eat straw just like the bull. And the sucking child will certainly play upon the hole of the cobra, and upon the light aperture of a poisonous snake will a weaned child actually put itsown hand.

They will not do any harm or cause any ruin in all my holy mountain, because the earth will certainly be filled with the knowledge of Jehovah asthe waters are covering the very sea.

I expected this stance to be met with the strongest resistance, that I would be teased and hounded, so it was to my amazement that it was accepted without question. They knew. And it would not again become a viable issue until nearly two more years had passed.

Long grown, my daughter had moved to Philadelphia the last day of February. It was 1988 and I experienced three spring times that year, the first when I visited Jeannine right outside the city line at which the Pennsylvania countryside immediately begins. It was early April, and Dicey and I were going to Ireland at the end of the month, where I would again enjoy the soft air and pink-and-white blossoms surrounding me now. I have never quite grown accustomed to having to wait well into May for this yearly spectacle in Massachusetts. That year, I was more than happy to be welcomed by it on our return from overseas.

Somewhere in the few weeks between Pennsylvania and Ireland, we noticed that Ches seemed to be getting a bit thin. Nothing to be alarmed about at that point, we were sure, but we would keep an eye open; and if it continued by the time we got back, a consultation with the vet would be in order.

As Dicey and I drove from Limerick to Killarney, down through Skibbereen, along the South Coast to Cork City, where we renewed acquaintances with old friends, on to Dublin, and finally, across to Galway and Connemara, our beautiful golden cat was never far from our minds.

Home again, one look at our once lovely Ches answered any question we could have asked. Ches was very, very sick, and we knew that he was dying. Jeannine had come up to cat-sit for us.

"I didn't want to call and alarm, you, Ma. He just went downhill fast, and I only hoped he would last until you two got here."

"You did the right thing."

The vet confirmed our worst suspicions.

"Leukemia. It is a virus that they can pick up and carry around for years. He probably contacted it while he was fending for himself, trying to find his way home. I recommend that you let me put him to sleep."

"Do it now Good-bye, love."

"I also recommend that you have all the rest of your cats tested."

What good would it do? If they've got it, we will know soon enough.

"You should also be sure that you bring no new cats into your house for at least two years."

Yes, *and while we're at it, we will also make sure that the moon nolonger shines and that pigs learn how to fly.*

China Doll

Jo Jo was so proud, and purring so contentedly when we first discovered her golden treasures, that we put aside our impulse to pick them up and brush our cheeks against their soft little bodies. So as not to upset their mother, that would come later. She gave no early sign of leaving them, even momentarily, so our resistance and consideration were short-lived. First one, then another, lovingly caressed and examined. Then—stop—look—what's that underneath number three?

Oh, no! Please don't let it be so, as I lifted the lifeless form of the most exquisitely beautiful kitten that I had ever seen, or, I believe, I ever will see. Much smaller than the rest, fur of down rather than fuzz, I turned the limp little neck to behold a face that only a very loving Creator could design—tiny pink nose on a white face, etched with black around the eyes. Orange and black patches on white quickly revealed her to be a calico, or, a money cat, our first and only, but to me, the dainty delicate features and perfect markings were those of an expertly crafted china doll. This was the only side of her that was visible to us then; we saw no evidence at all of the little terror that she would become, or that one day, poor old Idi would run for his life at the sight of her.

At that moment, I had no doubt at all that she was dead and the joy of discovering her melted as my heart sank. Still, it was impossible not to hold and stroke her while whispering to her who-knows-what little nothings.

Wait a minute. Look closely—carefully. Did she move ever so slightly? I felt rather than heard the little sigh that made my heart leap. Undersize to begin with, she was weakened from lying beneath the other little pigs who had evidently greedily edged her away from her mother's breasts. This mistreatment now corrected, she was soon nursing right along with the rest.

Jo Jo was a wonderful mother and one of the wonders that we would not have missed was to watch her expertly teach her babies how to stand up and walk.

The boys were promised early, and Goldie was claimed by my mother; and it was only the little doll's future that was uncertain.

"You'll have no trouble finding a home for her. She is so beautiful, anyone would want her."

You would certainly think so, but-with those to whom she was offered, such was not the case. Good, dear friends, who loved cats, who would have given her a wonderful home, expressed interest—half-heartedly. They came to see her several times, and what at first appeared to be love at first sight was wrongly assessed. They were holding back, and though we never asked, we later wondered if they had sensed a hesitation on our part to let her go. Whatever the case, we took the initiative a few days before they were to give us their final decision, to announce that she was no longer available. No hard feelings, no strain in the friendship, only good wishes. Shortly thereafter, they found their beloved Ruby, a stray kitten badly in need of their love. File under "Somehow Things Work Out for the Best."

It was not long after the movie "10" had peaked in popularity. Not having seen it, to this day I do not know the name of the fictional character portrayed by Ms. Bo Derek. The closest connection I could make was simply to name the cat "Bo."

"Why Bo?"

"Cause she's a ten. Besides, she looks like a 'Bo.' As she grew and the beauty of her features intensified, her name seemed incomplete. Whose name could be added to aptly enhance this little creature? Who else's but that of the woman whose face could still be her fortune and who, in my opinion, will always be the Most Beautiful Woman in the World? Who also bears what, in my opinion, is the most beautiful female name, a name perfectly fitted both to herself and to my cat?

In the first few weeks of her life, Bo Elizabeth, along with Goldie and the boys, grew. They were lively, frisky kittens. From the beginning, she and Goldie were as close as any twins, despite no resemblance in looks or personality. To *see* one was to see the other. Goldie gravitated toward Nana, though at night she found my bed. Bo was never off me day or night. In waking hours she would make the climb from my foot to my shoulder where her chin would rest while riding around in my arm. Pliable as putty, Bo always stayed wherever I put her, including my right armpit where she slept without moving through the night. And she drooled.

"Disgusting," says my husband.

Even though it was another I was to refer to as "my baby," Bo is the only cat I've ever spoken to in baby talk. "She's my pwincess."

"Disgusting."

Like Spot, Bo, too, was a water baby, but unlike him, she had never gone to the beach. His excursions had been halted, and mine also came to an end following the infamous Blizzard of '78. Debris littered our shores for months, even years afterward. Besides, as the tempo of life quickened, I no longer had time for the swims that had been almost a ritual. My time in the water was confined to soaks in the tub when either Spot or Bo, or both, would sit on the edge, dipping a paw, or splashing a tail, sometimes taking the complete plunge to be with me. In time, baths were replaced more and more with showers when Bo would sit outside the curtain snatching at every move I made. One day she sat there quietly. "I see you, Bo" was all the encouragement she needed. I squealed in delighted disbelief as the curtain flew open and a kitten who couldn't care less about getting soaked leaped onto my slippery body. Independent cats, unable to show devotion.

While the others are gone, Bo Elizabeth, at age twelve is vigorously alive and healthy today. She gave us our share of fright along the way.

As in so many families beginning.—when? In the seventies? The eighties? Increasing complex activities, conflicting schedules, kids growing up, running here, racing there—our one-time traditions became victims of the times. Everyone eating together at the dining-room table became a rare occasion. Dicey was in New Bedford, my mother took to eating at a TV table in the living room, Jeannine often ate "out," and I, sometimes, didn't eat at all.

Nana was in her armchair, head bowed, eyes closed in prayer. On the tray in front of her sat a plate of spaghetti, smothered in a rich tomato sauce brimming with sausages, onions, and green peppers. Sneaking up behind her on the left side was a light-footed pussycat, nose twitching at the tantalizing aroma. I was only passing through and did not stand still to watch. Either my mother was going into lengthy detail in giving thanks, or she had dozed off, because the next time I glanced their way, her eyes were still closed, and there was Bo, rear feet on the arm of the chair, furry little "hands" tugging at the spaghetti like a robin in the garden. From the smudges of tomato on the tiny face, she had already eaten some of it and evidently couldn't get enough.

Replacing Nana's dinner, I then made the mistake of preparing a small portion of sausage and peppers for Bo in her own dish on the floor. This meal was met with such relish, that for the next ten days, until she nearly died of self-imposed starvation, Bo made it very clear that she would eat only Italian food. A hunger strike was on, one that was to leave us drained from grief and anxiety. Cat food was out of the question. Even the smell of it seemed to sicken her. We bought chicken, boiled and chopped it, ground sirloin—and well done, ham and turkey from the deli the best "people" tuna we could buy. Nothing brought any response except minced-up pieces of oven-heated frozen pizza.

"You are killing her," blamed the vet over the phone. "A kitten's system cannot digest that kind of food; besides, it contains none of the nutrients she needs."

There was no question that she was dying. Day by day she was growing weaker. The bright, beautiful fur became dull and colorless. Goldie became noticeably larger while Bo's eyes closed, and she was no longer strong enough to stand on her feet.

In the vet's office, in desperation: "Isn't there ANYTHING you can do?"

"No. You've got to do it. Stop giving her junk food. Give her nothing. She will not starve herself. You've got to show her who's the boss, that she MUST eat what YOU give her. Stop allowing her to manipulate you. She is only a kitten."

Stern, no-nonsense advice, hard to deal with, but what choice did we have? There was little left to lose. Hope nearly gone, we tried it the vet's way. The next morning, Bo accepted an ever-so-tiny portion of tuna. At the next feeding time, she took a little more, then a little more. Within a couple of days, she began to revive. *Thank God.*

As you might guess, from that day forward, Bo was hooked on tuna fish, a steady diet of which is not particularly in a cat's best interests, but in her case, no negative effects have been evident in all of these twelve years. In time, she accepted cat tuna and will occasionally condescend to a small taste of roast beef or turkey from our leftovers.

What has remained with us from this experience is that, regardless of size or importance, or its apparent lack of significance as it fits into the overall scheme of things, it is possible for any living creature to display a will of iron.

The Gentleman

I first became aware of the cat who was to become "Little Kitty" back in the early seventies, when we would occasionally meet up with this tough-looking ragamuffin roving around, looking out of place in a neighborhood where animals, for the most part, were well-cared for. Once every two or three months, or so, he would show up on the back doorstep, and I would give him some scraps from our own cats' leftovers. We knew that, to some extent, he was cared for elsewhere, but not by any means was he anyone's cherished pet. He had the usual earmarks of an unaltered tom, including nicked ears, scratches on his nose, and missing chunks of fur from various parts of his body. It was not until after the Blizzard of '78 that we learned who "owned" him and his supposed name, which we were told was "Boots."

"But he only comes home about once a month, so he isn't *really* our cat."

Up until that time, if I saw him within any reasonable distance of our house or yard, I would call out in my shrillest peal—"Little Kitty"—and he would make his way over for a meal or a snack. Any attempt on my part to show him friendship met with embarrassed resistance.

Every Cat Person knows that cats can smile when they choose to, but I believe that even if Little Kitty wanted to, he would not have been able. This was a serious cat and remained so throughout his long life. Even the stiff set of his neck was serious. There was no play in him, and it was hard to imagine that he had ever been a kitten. This was a pirate escaped from a ship. Captain Hook himself minus the eye patch and triangular hat.

By the time the blizzard struck, even if Little Kitty still had eight and a half of his lives left, and one half seemed more likely, they would not have carried him through that catastrophe. Thankfully, we saw him shortly before it broke; and sensing that this storm meant business, I brought him into the house where he spent the next ten days in our cellar. Our cats would never have associated with such low life; and as it was, we had to put up with their hissing and bewildered faces every time they passed the cellar door.

When the flooding and snowdrifts finally began to subside, and the U.S. Army pulled out after guarding what had turned into our island for nearly two weeks, we let Little Kitty outdoors to go about his business. It was at this moment that a young girl who lived beyond the bend in the road said, "Oh, you've had our cat. We were wondering where he was." It was then that I learned his name, along with the remark that he "wasn't really" their cat. I will not make comment on what I thought of their care of him, because in all fairness, without intending to, by this lime, I, too, had a parttime ownership of him. People seeing him come out of my house could have the same opinion of me as I had of those who claimed him. Neglectful.

As the years went by, Little Kitty continued to visit us as the mood struck. I'd prefer to call his manners "abrupt" rather than rude; he simply had no understanding of affection, and I doubted he had ever been shown any.

Looking back, I will always be glad that he knew where to come when he was in real trouble. One late winter morning in 1982, he arrived on my doorstep, beaten up almost to the point of mutilation, obviously from a very vicious cat fight. Tom, bleeding, dirty, and ugly, he did not protest when we wrapped him up and made a hurried trip to the animal hospital. From that day onward, he was no longer a partially owned stray. Like it or not, he was our cat.

Compassion aside, it dawned on me that the lady vet was looking at me rather strangely. After all, she was used to seeing every cat I ever brought in being bright eyed and clean, if not necessarily bushy tailed. And no getting around it, Little Kitty looked nasty. Before making arrangements to have him "fixed," as well as healed, I reminded him: "I don't love you; in fact, I don't even particularly like you. And I'm definitely not your mother."

I am ashamed of myself now, but this was not a cat who inspired any kind of maternal instinct. I could, perhaps, in time be his friend, as well as his benefactor, but never would I be his mother. Little did I know of the role reversal in store for us, that he would become my self-appointed surrogate father. When Little Kitty came home, all cleaned up and manicured, he looked about as comfortable as a person who had lived in rags on the streets for years being suddenly snatched up, showered, shaved, and dressed in a tuxedo. Though definitely out of character, he was willing to go along with the game and reasonably content to stay indoors throughout his full recuperation and transition.

"This is it, Little Kitty. Now or never. We'll get to know each other; and if love never develops, at least we can coexist with respect."

I will give him all the credit that he deserved for making the adjustment. Although it was certainly not a precondition to his permanent residence at 20 Chapel Street, I believe he felt it was necessary to outgentleman every other male in the house. Did they give him behavior therapy in the hospital? All I know is what I saw as aloofness became attentiveness and indifference became concern.

Casual acknowledgment OF became obsession WITH me. His attachment was as close as if our ankles had been chained together; and from that time onward, for the rest of his life, whether I was sitting, standing, sleeping—upstairs or downstairs—in the house or in the yard, or walking down the street, Little Kitty was at my side. He never was able to express love in the form of affection, but no loyalty and devotion from one creature to another could have exceeded what he gave to me. To the very limits of his abilities, Little Kitty was my guardian.

The years passed, and it was one winter when Little Kitty came to another crisis in his life. Jeannine and I were in the dining room. As usual, Little Kitty not far from my feet. The first clue that something was wrong came when he began going around in a circle, as if chasing his tail. This was not our Lord of the Manor, who would never stoop to anything so undignified as play. Eyes rolled back in his head, he came to a standstill, stiffened, and fell over on his side; he appeared to be dead. Little Kitty had had a stroke. We had little hope, nor, as it appeared, did the vet from Australia who seemed more intent on paperwork and asking questions regarding the cat's early medical history, for which we had no answers, than attending to him. Yet, no one wanted to bring up the subject of "putting him to sleep."

Silently, I wrestled with my conscience. Few are more critical than I when it comes to people who allow their animals to suffer, yet, as with Mary, I again felt I made the right decision. Something about the little body, even though now covered with silky fur in place of matted hair, was still tough and sturdy. Whether he recovered or not, Little Kitty was coming home.

It took a long, long time, and I'm sure there are some who felt I was cruel and thought that he was suffering; but knowing him as well as I did and being with him every day, I wouldn't agree. There was little that we could do for him except to keep water nearby and coax him in and out of the litter box. But everyone's patience was finally rewarded. After a month, Little Kitty could stand up on his own; in two months, he was wobbling around; in three, he was back to normal; and by late spring, he was strong and healthy, ready to go outdoors again.

One night, well into the early hours of the morning, Jeannine was driving her convertible down the street. Next to her, in the passenger's seat was Little Kitty.

"All right, where did you pick him up?"

Coming down the street, she glanced under a street-light at a group of cats from Little Kitty's old gang. He was in their midst; and it appeared they were getting ready to tackle him when she stopped the car, scooped him up, and brought him home.

"Now, Ma, I'm afraid they're all going to be saying he's a sissy. He'll never be able to face them again." *Good.*

As my father used to say, "Time waits for no one." Little Kitty had three happy, healthy years after his stroke, and his slowdown was gradual. In his last days, he slept on my pillow, close to my head, but, sadly, I was not with him at the end. He never had another sick day, but one night I came home from work and found him under my bed.

Jeannine had always expressed a certain scorn for Little Kitty; and perhaps it was a touch of guilt or regret, but she offered the jacket of her pink silk suit for him to be buried in. So, he left the world in a much better style than that in which he had apparently entered it.

One For You...

Other One For Jo Jo

If Mary was my Number One Girl and Bo my FAP (Feline American Princess), Tina was, and always will be, my Baby. Since her we've had five new kittens to again brighten our lives, to replace our tears with laughter, and to once more overfill our hearts with love. But none of them have taken her place. None ever will. She was the nearest to my heart and remains so in death, the only one I have ever thought of, perhaps wrongly, as my child.

Not that she ever did anything extraordinary, nor was she exceptionally pretty. She was just my baby. There was something about the pureness of her love that touched not only my heart, but my very life.

The pain on that day when I found her seared through every fiber of my being, matched only once before in my life on a daffodil-covered hill in Brooklyn when my husband revealed an event that would shatter our lives forever. Most of us have such moments, after which we are never again the same. Blessed are those who don't.

For Tina, her life began as it ended—in tragedy. It was November 1984. Jeannine found her a few miles from home, in the woods, in the rain. Cold, starving, alone, "the only one left of a litter dumped there," according to a neighborhood woman who "didn't know what happened to the rest of them." Concerned in an offhand kind of way, but enough to try to help any of them? Not by a long shot.

Short-haired, black, pointed ears and chin, long-legged and double-pawed she sat on Nana's lap. She had big eyes, much too serious for a kitten. Was she afraid of what we, too, would do to her? I held her closely.

"No one will ever hurt you again, Baby. You are safe now."

And she was, for as long as it was in my power to so keep her.

In time she blossomed, and how I loved to see the spindly little legs grow firm and strong as Tina Marie raced not only the length of the porches, but around the entire house. Some cats are noisy, some are quiet. Most "meow." Tina chirped. Whenever I came into the house, before I even put down my purse and parcels, I would call at the top of my voice, "TINA," and before her name left my lips, she would race to me, stop short, and chirp her greeting before leaping into my waiting arms.

Little habits developed that were Tina's alone. It took me a while to learn what was her favorite treat. "Nibbles" was the password and in time became one of her nicknames. We had our routine. "Do you want your nibbles, Baby?" was step one; step two was when she would jump up and tap me, and tap me; while at step three, I gave her a sample of one treat after another until she finally trained me to shake a few drops of cooking oil on the end of my finger and she lapped it off with her greedy little tongue, licking her chops in satisfaction.

Tina initiated the games, and what fun she had. So did I, but I was the one to tire first. She would get on my lap and sit facing me. I held her oversize front paws, and she would ease backwards and down, down on top of my legs, head hanging near the floor. And I would pull her up to starting position when the procedure would begin again. Down and up, down and up.

Toddlers do it all the time. The last time she was to do it, it was she who tired first and she fell asleep in my lap. I told myself that I was silly to feel so badly when I finally had to wake her up and put her down. I kissed her. "I'm sorry, Baby."

Her favorite game of all was to leap onto the highest perch in the room and sail through the air to land on my back. Stretching along my neck and shoulders, I would reach back and stroke and tickle her between little kisses until off she jumped. Turning around, she would be back on my shoulders in less than a moment. Back and forth, back and forth until, fool that I was, I began to think of myself as a landing pad. "Bat Girl" my husband called her. All she needed was a little black cape.

The trouble didn't start until her third year, and I believe that Tina thought this, too, was a game. The cats we have today manage to get out every once in a while, but three of them, at least, were street smart almost from birth. Tina was not. Especially since Jo Jo's calamity, we had been doubly cautious. Having no comprehension of the dangers lurking outside to any little animal, maybe it was just the fun of being chased that gave Tina so much enjoyment in sneaking out the back door and taking off as fast as her nimble legs could go. She wasn't too difficult to catch, and we always had her back in the safety of the house in a few minutes. But it became a worry. A huge German shepherd lived next door; and though we never saw Torro go after a cat, insofar as we could help it, we were not about to provide him with the kind of bait that might tempt him into changing his mind. Dear Torro, as it turned out, was not what we should have feared.

Along with our commuter marriage arrangement, Dicey and I maintained an apartment in New Bedford. It was spacious and provided a perfect backdrop for the entertaining that we loved to do, as well as fitting in perfectly with our work-home-travel schedule. By that time, my mother, too, was living in an apartment in the same complex. Two years earlier, Nana had broken her hip in six places, mending and recovering almost miraculously. The doctors had not held out any hope that, at age eighty-seven, she would ever be able to live a normal life at home again, consigning her, in fact, to the bed with five minutes a day for sitting in a chair.

"She belongs in a nursing home," they said. "There is no way you could possibly take care of her."

She had stopped eating, and I don't believe any of the hospital personnel expected her to live for very long. Returning to the cottage was out of the question. Her eyesight was failing, and aside from the dangers of stumbling over the cats, our impossible task would have been keeping her off the stairs, especially those going into the cellar.

"She will come to New Bedford with me," said Dicey. 'And before you know it, she will be back to herself again." "That is very doubtful, sir"

In three months, Nana was on her feet, eating like a truck driver, and living in her own apartment in the adjacent building.

It is easy to condemn a parent who, in a department store, turns his or her head for a moment, during which second a child disappears, perhaps forever. Or the one whose child breaks loose and dashes into the street only to be struck by a speeding vehicle. There was the well-publicized case of the child who fell into a well. "Where was the mother?" is the question echoed from every direction; condemnation first, facts established afterward. There is no living thing that can be watched without distraction for twenty-four hours a day, unless it is a creature held captive for that very purpose.

Dicey and I were in New Bedford, doing our own and my mother's fall cleaning on the November weekend when the call came from Jeannine.

"Does Tina have a hiding place? I haven't seen her today."

As a matter of fact, she had taken to sleeping under my downstairs bed, and lately I had more and more been finding her in the same spot. It was only the night before that I had leaned under there to say good-bye to her.

"She's not there, Ma. I can't find her anyplace."

"We will be home."

The hour's drive was interminable. *Hurry up. No. Slow down.* The roads are treacherous. The first winter storm of the season had left patches of snow and ice. *Hurry, we've got to find her. Take your time. She is gone.*

Jeannine had searched every nook and cranny of the neighborhood, as she had for Jo Jo—to no avail. This time there was no way I could have rested until I had retraced her steps myself. My heart cries out for every parent who has ever searched for a missing child. Hope is a torment that ebbs and flows like the tide that dangles and torments.

Exhausted with the fear of not knowing what I would discover, throat raw from calling, by midnight my head finally touched the pillow, but not for long. By 2:00 A.M. I was ready to return to the street.

"You are crazy," said my family.

Mr. Benson had awakened and seen our lights. His dear, concerned face peered in our back door. "I will help you," he said. For another hour we looked, flashlights in hand, he in one direction, I in another. Nothing. Despair set in as I returned to bed.

"We will find her in the morning," said Dicey.

No. She is gone.

I had known it from the very first ring of the phone. The morning sun returned beauty and bright color to the world around us, but not to our heavy hearts. After a fitful sleep, my first awareness was of the task that we could not yet put to rest.

Jeannine dressed ahead of me. "I am going to speak to some of the neighbors. Maybe someone has seen her."

She was back before I could leave to make my own daylight search. Dicey had returned to New Bedford.

"The pool, Ma."

Oh, no. Please, dear Father.

"Mrs. Dunn looked out her window and caught a glimpse of something black. She couldn't look any farther. Neither could I. But we know it is her. One of the boys will get her out for you."

"NO! NO!" I don't even remember how I got out the door, through the yard, into theirs, through the door to their patio. Then I was down on my face, coat off, stretching, reaching, pounding, hitting the ice, grabbing, until the frozen little body was in my arms. First I screamed, then the sobs came as I rocked her and held her close to my heart.

Either out of respect for my agony and feeling that giving me my privacy was best, or fear of a woman gone demented, or both, I don't know, but no one came near me. Even Jeannine retreated to our house.

Somehow, I made it to Mr. Benson's door.

"Eddie, I've found my Baby," came through the tears that streamed from my eyes. He did not say a word but motioned to one of the two chairs that stayed on his back porch summer and winter. I sat in one and he in the other; and there we remained until, I am sure, there was not another tear left to be shed. The sun warmed her fur, melting the ice, and I stroked her as I did when she was alive. My coat was still around her. Had the temperature risen so that I didn't need it, or was I too numb to feel the cold? The man from the electric company arrived to read the meter. He lowered his head in embarrassment as he passed, asking no questions. Perhaps an hour went by, maybe less. I was conscious of little but the warmth from the sun. God's comfort.

"I will dig a grave any place you want it," said Mr. Benson.

"In the front garden, please, as near to the house as possible."

I wrapped her in a small clean blanket. Mr. Benson kissed the little bundle before I lowered it into the cold earth.

Throughout the years, how many times I have heard that "it was only a cat." Nothing that the Maker sees fit to bestow with the gift of life is "only." Not wanting to hear it again, I kept my grief to myself.

"She was three years old, just beginning her life," I lamented to Jeannine.

"At least she had a life, Ma. Think of those who don't." It was of no consolation to me.

Two months later, Dicey gave me a long-stemmed red rose for our anniversary. Jeannine had been given a white one, for what occasion, I do not know. While still fresh, I placed them both on the little grave.

"One for you, Baby, and one for Jo Jo."

The Jersey Girls

He first contact I had with one of the Jersey girls was news of her adoption into a family of friends.

Contemplation of her acquisition began on a frigid winter's weekend of 1981. I was in Newark for an overnight visit with Rolland and Shirley Jones and the kids. Literally frozen in, travel to my next destination was canceled, and there was something of a lull in the conversation, which never veered very far from the weather. Excitement came in the form of Shirley making the stereotypical jump onto a chair by a frightened female, startled by the intrusion of a furry creation other than the feline variety.

"Ro, we've got to get another cat!"

Ro looked resigned as he nodded in agreement. Not a cat lover to begin with, he had had his fill with Prudence, the Siamese, who for years had followed their daughter from room to room, hollering at the top of her high-pitched voice during every waking hour.

"They aren't all like Pru."

A few weeks later, news came of the arrival of Tiffany. The Jones` didn't have long to wait or far to go for a kitten.

A pregnant mother cat wandered into a neighbor's yard and gave birth to a litter in their shed. The short-haired black female turned out to be Tiffany. I didn't meet her until the following year when the only brief thought I gave her was that she somehow reminded me of Goldie. I also noted that she looked like Ron, the young Jones girl's suitor. I was not the only one to make the observation, but was a bit surprised to find my opinion to be commonly held among our circle of friends. Ron is a black man and Tiffany is a black cat, but this fact is incidental. Tiffany bore features of Goldie; Goldie is yellow. Tiffany and Ron share shape of face, the set of their large, perceptive eyes, high cheeks, and narrow chins.

"There is nothing more disgusting than comparing a human being to an animal. You ought to be ashamed of yourselves—all of you. Please don't ever say such a thing again."

This was before my husband had ever seen Tiffany and even much longer before he was to meet Ron.

Back in New Jersey in 1982, a young father named Walter wanted to introduce his youngsters to the joys of playing with a kitten. Selected kitten in hand, he headed for home with his furry surprise. They were not to make it. The next light of day seen by Walter was from a hospital bed.

"Where's the cat?" "What cat?" "Where's the car?"

"Towed to the junkyard."

After exiting the hospital, Walter's first stop was at the junkyard where, frightened, but unharmed, a tiny gray female kitten huddled under the front seat of the totaled car.

"A miracle," said Walter.

"A what?" said his wife.

"It stays."

"We'll see."

Walter and the kitten had the house to themselves while wife and children barricaded themselves in the bedroom.

On day three, the bell rang at the Jones's residence. As the door was opened, a gray kitten sailed unceremoniously through the air into the front hall as Walter made a hasty retreat. So much for the battle of wills. The kitten had lost—or had she?

The explanation for a new kitten in the Jones's household: Walter's wife was afraid of it. Afraid of a cat? Hard to understand, but everyone has their fears, explicable and otherwise, but afraid of a kitten? Now I'd heard it all. But I hadn't seen "it" yet. It's a wonder the poor little beggar wasn't named "What's that?"

Shirley was making a bed when I got my first glimpse of Yoda. I hated my own meanness as the little monster with a face that only a mother could love peeped from behind the spread.

"Shirley, you *know* that thing is going to talk to you—and its language will be neither cat nor human."

Normal-size body, short little legs, twitching tail, the self-assured puss just knew she was the fairest of them all. But it was the face, which, if any of us ever exploited her, probably would have brought in a fortune. Supermarket mag material: "Space Alien Living in Newark."

As if made of Silly Putty, it was not just the pressed-in face of a Persian or a Himalayan; it also appeared to have been turned to the side. The nose sat on sideways, slanted in the same direction as the rest of the face, and there was a dent at the top of her nose. Eyes bulged and ears tilted to the side rather than straight up. The upper and lower jaws did not match, so a little red tongue would hang perpetually from between crooked teeth. Precious, ugly, darling baby.

It was 1985 when Jeannine approached me. Wandy and Ron were getting married. They couldn't have the cats in the apartment where they would live. Ro and Shirley were moving. The cats would not be going with them to their new home.

"Are they going to be driven up, or are you going down to get them?"

"I've already made my reservations."

Months later, a progress report was sent in the form of two letters.

As far as cats go, Ro and my husband both claim to belong to the I-Wouldn't-Hurt-Them-But-I'd-Just-As-Soon-Not-Have-Them-Around-and-I-Can't-Really-Understand-What-You-People-See-In-Them group.

Our commuter marriage was still in operation, and he saw them only on weekends, so my husband did not qualify to be a full-time daddy. I could not resist rubbing it in Ro's face:

Dear Wandy, Shirley, Derry, and DADDY, I miss you most of all, Daddy, because I have a new mommy and lots of new sisters and brothers, but no daddy!

It is very very hard to admit, but I think maybe someday I just might get to like my new mommy. My sister Jeannine put Yoda and me in my grandmother's room as soon as we arrived here from New Jersey. I made sure she and Mommy knew from the beginning that I hated their guts, so I spit at them every chance I got. I thought that maybe if I refused to eat they might send me back to my real family, but after three days, my hunger just took over.

Mommy kept coming in every morning and every night, trying to talk to me, telling me she loves me and that everything will be all right. We'll see!

After the first ten days, whenever she came in, I started out to be nice to her then remembered she wasn't Wandy and really spit at her bad. She said, "That's all right. I have lots of patience and I love you." So even though I didn't trust her for a minute, about a week ago, I decided to stop spitting at her. After all, why waste my spit? Now she leaves the door open so I can come out and look around.

The other day, I actually came halfway down the stairs, but when Mommy said to come all the way, I decided to be spiteful and ran back to my room again. Sometimes I go under my sister Jeannine's bed, but mostly I just peek at everybody. Fresh little Freddie and nosy little Tina keep sneaking into my room. Freddie thinks he owns the place, even though he came here just a week before we did. Jeannine brought him home too, just like Tina last year. Jeannine brings everybody home! Like Mommy says, maybe someday we'll all be friends!

Love, Tiffy

Dear Wandy, Shirley, Deny, and DADDY,

Even though I wasn't very happy about taking that plane ride and coming here with all these new folks, I decided from the beginning that I wouldn't lose anything by being just a little bit nice. I was very, very scared, but I only spit a little bit at my new mommy and sister Jeannine— not like Tiffy who spits at them ALL the time!

I used to hide under my grandmother's sewing basket and I still will not go out of the room on my own, but when Mommy or Jeannine carry me out, I don't mind. It's even kind of nice once in a while. Jeannine takes me into bed with her and I've got her well trained. All I have to do is holler my head off, and she will come get me and cuddle me. The only trouble is—everybody sleeps in Jeannine's bed.

Mommy has tried to take me downstairs with my new brothers and sisters, but I dig my claws real hard into her, so she says, 'All right. I won't force you," so then I get to stay in bed with Jeannine. Mommy sleeps downstairs, so I don't get to sleep with her (unless someday I decide to be brave enough to go down), but I love to jump on her back when she comes into my room.

I was a very bad girl last week when Mommy wanted to take me to the doctor to get my stitches out. A lady was waiting outside in the car and I made Mommy chase me all over the house while I ran up and down the stairs and under the sofas and beds. That time, I spit at her as much as Tiffy does! It was so much fun making

her run that I forgot how scared I am of coming out of my room! I was a good girl after the first five minutes in the car, and I enjoyed all the attention from everyone in the doctor's office; but, why were they all staring at me and wondering what I was?

Freddie came with us that day and we were both very good getting our shots, but Freddie ran all over the doctor's office while I stayed still like a good girl.

Love Yoda

A few months later, at a pre-wedding gathering in New Jersey, scores of young black men were circulating. No introductions were necessary. Dicey needed no one to point out the future bridegroom. "You are not going to believe this, but I know which one is Ron."

The Upstairs Girl

"Atherine she should have been called," out of the blue from my husband the other day.

"Who?"

"You know, the lady who played in all those movies with Spencer Tracey."

"Hepburn."

"Yes—sophisticated, poised, in control— beautiful."

Katherine Hepburn is called Katherine. What is he getting at? Does he mean no one should refer to her as "Kate?" Were they discussing it on TV?

The cat had already left the room before I realized he was saying we should have called this lovely, nameless creature after a female who possessed all the same characteristics.

It was January of 1986, on a particularly brutal night, when the all-too-often-repeated chain of events ended with another new cat in our lives.

"Ma, I promise I'll find a home for her."

You already did. Just like all the others.

"We can't leave her outside in this freezing weather."

"Of course we can't." Besides, I knew the moment I laid eyes on her that she would stay.

Jeannine: "Do you realize that we have twelve cats now?"

Yes.

I also knew it would not be for long. Spot was going downhill and, as it turned out, lived only a couple more weeks. Jo Jo was getting frail, and I was hoping she would make it to the spring.

"All right. Let's have the story."

This was not your usual throw-away. Well-bred and mannered, someone had cared for her and, I am sure, felt the pain of her loss. But who? And where? For how long and to what extent can you disrupt your own life to track down what may never be found? In this case, the procedures had already been followed. A girlfriend of Jeannine's had found the cat wandering the streets of a neighboring town ten miles or so to our south, a few nights earlier, at the start of this cold snap. She already had two cats of her own, which had been allowed to stay only grudgingly by a reluctant stepfather. Doors had been knocked on, ads placed, calls made to shelters, with negative results. She was given the ultimatum: "The cat can go or you and the cat can go, your decision.

What would anyone with a heart do? The choices are few throw it back out in the cold, take it to the pound where it would be kept for twenty-four hours, or find-someone-with-a-mother-who-will-let-it-stay.

The cat had green eyes and a wide face, with muddled markings of black, white, and orange. White covering, the contour of each little toe, gave her feet the look of being star-tipped.

"Twinkle

Toes?" No, it was too cute for her personality. Perhaps if she had been a kitten, being with us may have helped her develop into a Twinkle Toes type. Actually, no name seemed to suit her

Where was my husband's insight then? We always tried to avoid those cat names that we've heard a hundred times: Mittens, Muffin, Frisky. Fluffy, and Jo Jo (which we since learned to be the most popular of cats' names) had been etched in stone long before their bearers had come to us. We've even tried to avoid the clever, original names we've occasionally heard other people give their cats. We like to think we can do it on our own.

She had class, she was intelligent, and she knew how to be persuasive.

She was also loud.

At the time, we told ourselves that she was afraid, and maybe she was. But an honest backward appraisal forces me to admit that we were probably just soft enough to allow her to dupe us. For an entire year, one or the other of us carried food, water, and the scooper upstairs, not once, but however many times a day necessary. Because this lady refused, under any circumstances, to come down. It was not long before we labeled her "The Upstairs Girl," and though she eventually joined the downstairs peasants, to this day, she answers to what has been the only name we've ever given her.

The Other Woman

It was 1988. It was still May. Earlier in the month, Dicey and I had returned from Ireland. Ches had been gone for about a week. We were in New Bedford when there was a knock at our apartment door. We looked at each other. It was dinnertime. We had buzzed no one in.

"Who?"

A family of friends—mother, father, child, and . . . No, not this time. We've had more than our fill. They had been to New Hampshire on a brief vacation. They had passed a sign: "Free Kittens." This was the one they brought home, the one their landlord forbade them to keep.

"You've got to take it. If you don't, it will go to the pound. You know what will happen then. " said the father. The child's eyes were large.

How many times Dicey's voice in making a decision began with: "I'll see how Joyce feels about it." Admirable, considerate, unpresumptuous.

But not now, Dicey. This one is all yours. I gave him a neutral gaze and stood silently as I wondered how he would wriggle his way off the spot that he had been put on. I looked at the child. Was she crying? Did we understand how they felt? Only too well. But I'm glad I didn't weaken. Whatever the outcome, it would never be thrown in my face. Moments seemed like hours. Was I hearing things? No, it was Dicey saying to the man, "Well, I guess GRANNY could use a cat to keep her company. She lives alone in her apartment."

Granny, my foot! You can fool them, but you can't fool me, Dicey. We both know Granny could just as easily trip on a cat here as she could back in the cottage.

These people must have known us better than we thought they did. They had come prepared. Though their thanks were profuse, they did not linger. . . "and here is her dish and a brand-new litter box" The little girl had wanted to name the kitten "Kathy." I was willing, but Dicey had other plans. His cat, I mean Granny's cat, was going to be named Spooky— Spooky Louise. She and Granny would share the same middle name. Only Granny had no say whatsoever in the matter.

"Lou" appeared to be around six weeks old. Short-haired, steel gray, with a white patch on her chest, dainty, prim, her little personality was already formed. Although she would live in our apartment, there was no reason why she couldn't visit Nana once in a while as long as either Dicey or I were there. Only recently had animals been allowed here, and I had noticed my mother looking wistfully at other people's cats and dogs. I knew she deeply missed the cats at Chapel Street. It had crossed my mind to send The Upstairs Girl down to keep Dicey company during the week. Nana would be thrilled to meet Lou, to once more have a kitten to cuddle.

From my days in New York coaxing strays out of hiding, gaining their confidence and eventually their love, I had never known a cat that didn't respond to kindness and caring. Examples right in my own household included Little Kitty as well as the transients who would visit our door for an occasional meal and stay around for a while before moving on. And I never knew any animal that didn't warm to my mother. We had not yet encountered Lou.

"Come and see Nana, sweetheart," was greeted with bared teeth and claws.

"Pffft." *I'm not your sweetheart.*

An attempt by me to pet her brought the same reaction. *I'm not yoursweetheart either.*

If she had been human, we would have been questioning whether we used the right toothpaste.

Hostility, your name is Lou.

People-Who-Don't-Like-Cats, your reason is Lou.

Aggressive, defensive behavior is to be expected from an animal ravaged by cruelty or starvation, even one that has been spoiled and pampered over a number of years. But this was a baby, a nasty little kitten who chose for herself from the moment she laid eyes on him whose cat she would be and who she would claim for herself.

And how well I understood the magnetism of my husband's charm. I, too, was a baby when I fell under its spell, when I gave him my fifteen-year-old heart.

With him, Lou is affectionate, possessive, obedient, all of these things.

Never before had I seen firsthand, in my own life, a female so obsessed.

. . . Or had I? The years roll back to that long-ago time on Staten Island when, at five years old, my father was the center of my life, that is, when I didn't have to share him with Minnie.

Mean, even fierce, this spitfire of a tiger cat lived at his store, where a rodent had better not have even thought of entering her territory. It was a distance of two miles with at least half-a-dozen corners to turn and one main road to cross between our house and the store. Rain, shine, snow, cold—my father made the trip by foot. His alarm was synchronized with

Minnie's inner clock, because she would be at the same midway point to meet him every day.

Could I ever forget the moment he came into her view? The swift little feet would run, and she would jump to his shoulder where she remained for a ride back to the store.

There is where she stayed for most of the year, but the place was unheated in the winter when he would bring her home each night. At the store, we pretty much ignored each other as she and my father went about their respective business.

At home it was a different story. Here, she was off duty and my father's affection was to be undividedly hers. She was small and wiry, while our cats were huge. As soon as they knew she was in the house, they were nowhere to be found. At those times, even my mother, my sister, and I did not go near him. Conversations had to be held from one room to the next. I believe if we had come any closer, Minnie would have clawed our eyes out—or died trying. As for my father, no doubt such a display of female attention tickled his ego; or maybe he simply enjoyed being a wimp for a cat.

Their schedule did not change when Minnie was home. She would leave the house ahead of him to be waiting at their usual meeting place along the road.

Possessiveness was all that Lou had in common with Minnie. All other facets of their characteristics were vastly different. Minnie was a tough old lady. When not displaying her resentment of me, Lou is a little girl all the way. All of our paths, at one time or another, have been crossed by the obnoxious child that she so typifies. You know the kind— snooty, prissy little tattletales, who equate you with the speck of mud they wipe from their shiny little patent-leather shoes. The teacher's pet, the one set up on her own little pedestal to be better than all the rest.

I tolerated, even pitied the one in my class, who latched onto me for dear life. Underneath her fragile frills was a sad little person who couldn't understand why no one liked her. My pity of her extended beyond my dislike. I was no psychologist, and I was afraid if I told her the truth that she would shun me, and then she would really have no one. But I tried, in small ways to help her realize that she was only one in a sea of humanity, that others existed as well, that the world truly did not revolve around her. She was eventually sent to a "higher class" school, and I never saw her again; but it's hard not to remember her when I look at Lou.

It takes years to implant an attitude in a child, but the mystery remains as to how such haughtiness could be so mightily displayed in a kitten who had barely been weaned. Is it in the genes?

All I know is that from our first encounter, Lou made it clear that she wanted no part of me; she also wanted me to have no part of my husband. The presence of this creature filled the apartment in New Bedford, an apartment that I was glad was so large. Her vibes were almost tangible; and if the walls had been close around us, simply I would have smothered from her animosity. It is easier now that we are all together under one roof. The new house has many rooms and provides escape for us both. And there is the kitten who came last year, the kitten she oddly accepted as the only living soul besides my husband worthy of existence.

But I am getting ahead of myself. Then as now, her pursuit of Dicey's love was and is relentless. No trick in the book is left out from the blinking of her eyes to the swaying of her behind as she sashays around him, flirting outrageously, to the look in her face as she sits on his lap, as she lets me know in no uncertain terms that this is her man. Her eyes are never off him; and at any given time, they can be felt, if not seen, peaking at him, from under the pier table in the dining room, from the top of the refrigerator, from the top of the dresser.

Whether the sound of the car, or of his footsteps, Lou knows of Dicey's arrival. She can be in the deepest sleep and no matter who comes and goes along the street, the moment she hears him, the ears go up and the race is on to the door. His key no sooner turns in the latch when she is on his back, around his neck, purring, kissing, rubbing, swishing her tail in his mouth.

Bedtime is when I really feel that I am expected to pack my bags. It is bad enough when I walk from room to room and she attacks my ankles, spitting, growling, reaching out to trip me. Going up the stairs is a test as if by fire of just how much of her attempt at intimidation I will stand for before giving her a good swat. I haven't hit her yet. Fact is, I love her as much, no, not as much as the others, but enough to make room for her in my heart, if not in my lap. Lou and I do not share the bed with Dicey. In every other area of our lives within the house, she has made me to feel that I am The Other Woman in my own marriage, but not in the bedroom.

If you cannot sleep quietly at our feet, cat, then you've got to leave. You don't need to be shown or told. You know.

Lou would never sleep in the same bed with me any-way. When Dicey is working late into the night and I retire early, if Lou is in the bed, as soon as she sees me coming up the stairs, she will spit, growl, and be gone. The same when it is Dicey who lies down first and she with him. As soon as I enter the room, Lou departs, but not before making me aware of her displeasure.

And what is Dicey's role in this triangle? She is his "little tiny, tiny Lou" and how smug are her glares at me as he carries her in his arms like a baby. I do believe he derives enormous pleasure from being the center of this rivalry. It's been going on for years, but he stills gets a laugh every time I am away and call home. He puts the receiver with my voice coming through up to her ear.

"Say hello to your mama, Lou."

"*Sssss,* pffft," through the phone. This cat doesn't pass up a chance to let me know how much she hates me. I hear Dicey snickering in the background.

I also believe that Lou has become a convenience to him. He and she have become each other's mouthpiece as messages are passed to me that either one of them cannot give directly—Lou because she cannot speak, Dicey because . . . maybe he doesn't dare to.

He uses his best "Geraldine" voice. I had bought a new outfit and was not sure if Dicey would like it enough for me to wear to an upcoming event. One morning, I tried it on in the bedroom. They had already been up for a while. I slowly walked down, halfway hoping for a whistle—or some indication °this reaction. I didn't have to wait very long. They were both at the bottom of the stairs. First, silence, followed by Lou's growls.

"I'm not in the mood for her, Dicey: Please get her out of my way."

"Grrrr."

Dicey: "Say good morning to your mama, Lou."

Lou: "I don't want to say good morning to her. I hate her."

Dicey: "Why don't you tell her she looks nice?"

Lou: "I think she looks stupid."

Once, in New Bedford, Jeannine was visiting from Philadelphia. It was nearly time for her to leave when she noticed Lou ensconced on the wing-backed chair.

"That's a good chair, Ma. Make her get off."

"I do what I want to do—go where I want to go. This is my house, not yours."

"I don't know how you stand it, Ma," were my daughter's parting words as she slammed the door.

I had to agree with her about the chair and told Dicey so. Variations of those scenes could fill many more pages.

Lou still goes out of her way to get into and on top of places where she knows I do not want her to be.

"Dicey, she's only doing it to annoy me."

He says he doesn't think so, as she smirks at me. The only times when she has ever shown her willingness for a possible truce between us is when Dicey has been in the hospital. She senses that his absence at these times is somehow different and almost accepts me—for the moment. I wonder if her knowledge that she must now depend on me to be fed is also accompanied by a small fear that he might not be back.

And They Keep On Coming–the Later Years

The years had proceeded at a full and active, though orderly pace. Changes, when they began, came in swift succession, permanently altering our lives. They started with our loss of Ches and followed with our questionable gain of Lou. In the interim, a blessed event had taken place in the house next door. That family, too, had a "Spooky," only theirs was pregnant at every possible opportunity. I would occasionally notice whatever batch of kittens happened to be on hand at any given time; amazingly, they always managed to find homes with a seemingly endless supply of relatives. This well, too, was about to run dry.

Every night as I came through the yard, the call would come from Linda or her son, Frankie, or both, to see how "cute" was this latest trio of fur balls. I knew I was being primed and did my best to keep my eyes straight ahead. Cute they were as I caught a glimpse here and there of a g ray-stripe d male with white underneath and a gray-and-white female, both double pawed and bushy tailed. Then there was the black female, bushy tailed as well, all three long haired and fluffy. Only, it was where I saw them that I was trying to close my eyes to—in the glove compartment of their car, under their trunk, in the gutter.

Mind your business. They will soon have new homes.

It wasn't working. Mr. Benson echoed my fears.

"Frankie is too rough with those kittens. Linda is doing nothing about it. I hate to see it every day. Would you consider taking them? It would give Linda a break."

How about giving Joyce a break?

"No."

The summer progressed and so did the temperatures. One dog-day night as I came into the driveway, the scene was different. Linda was waiting for me by the fence; her arms were full, and so were her eyes. As I fumbled for my key, she said, "Will you take them?"

"Linda, bring them in before I change my mind." It was the heat. I had no other explanation to give to myself or to Dicey. Linda left without a word beyond, "Don't tell Frankie you've got them." Yes, in addition to taking them off her hands, I also agreed to keep it a secret.

What-have-I-gotten-myself-into-I'm-too-old-for-this-nowwe've-got-eleven-cats.

Too late for self-recrimination. Besides, I could no more send them back to where they came from than I could return them to their mother's womb.

They looked at me lovingly, trustingly. These were not shy, timid kittens. They were streetwise little urchins, who in the few short weeks of their lives had learned what a sheltered house cat would never need to know.

My first task was to get rid of the fleas and stickers and to cut off the knots from their matted coats, and then to pick out names for them. After much deliberation, it was Patrick for the boy, and Baby Jane for the black-haired girl. The second girl required no thought whatever. There was already a name waiting to be claimed by a gray-and-white cat, and the name was Clarissa. "Wiss" I call her, and though the feeling has been there for each new addition, it was especially for Clarissa that

I wondered how I ever considered my life to have been full without her.

Wiss sings, Wiss dances, and Wiss chatters. She is like a caricature— and calls to mind Disney-created cartoon cats from various times and places. And, like Tina, Baby Jane chirps and darts from here to there like a pixie. The three of them kept the cottage, and me, hopping that year; and once more, any would-be dull moments were quickly expunged.

Windows were open, summer floated through the house, and after the initial adjustment, life once more fell into routine for a short while.

Warmth lingered into September, and the leaves were showing their first patches of orange and red when word came from New Bedford that my mother had fallen. Her injuries were serious. She had a fractured left arm that resembled an elongated eggplant. Dicey had brought her to the emergency room where it was set, and hospitalization was not required. However, instructions were to be scrupulously obeyed if a full recovery was to be expected. She was to eat and move around as usual.

I guess she just gave up, or the pain was so severe that it obliterated reason from her mind. Dicey brought her back to the cottage when he came that weekend. Although she came with him occasionally, we all knew this time was different, and events fell into place to make her last visit home a happy memory, one that gives us no pain.

She and the cats were overjoyed to be with each other, and she was nearly smothered with their welcoming purrs and kisses. Goldie planted herself on Nana's lap, and there she stayed for hours at a time until Nana's knees grew numb. The new kittens were all a warm curiosity, and how I wished it had been one of these that had been in New Bedford instead of the hateful Lou. Those two days were about as perfect as they could be under the circumstances, except that my mother would eat nothing at all.

I will always see her in the front seat of the car on her way back with Dicey that Sunday night. The neighbors flocked around to give her brief hellos and good-byes. She smiled and waved to all of us as the car turned around the bend in the road.

I rarely went to New Bedford during the week and had not been given any alarm by Dicey to do so on the following Thursday night. The bus ride from Boston seemed to take forever. The face on the full moon was very clear that evening, and I felt it staring at me relentlessly as the bus crawled with the bumper-to-bumper traffic. There was a detour due to an accident. I almost didn't make it.

My mother was fine when I walked in the door. She was sitting on the sofa, smiling, and her pain appeared to have abetted. Lou jumped back and forth, giving us dirty looks, spitting at us. I was there for less than half an hour when my mother simply and peacefully took her last breath.

There was a large turnout for her funeral. The matchless glory of the early fall was nearly a distraction, the flowers more festive than funereal, the feast afterward one we all enjoyed, because we knew how much she would have enjoyed it. Finally, it was all over. Jeannine left for Pennsylvania, our cousins for New York. Dicey and I went back to the cottage to unwind. Patrick sat next to me on the sofa. A bobby pin fell out of my hair.

He snatched it with his huge paws and promptly popped it down his throat.

We had barely left the cemetery and had no plans to return there any time soon. My mother had been given an abundance of comforts and had lived a full and satisfying life, secure in the knowledge that she was well loved and cared for. Now she was at rest. But there we were, hours later, passing the spot, as we lost no time in getting Pat to the hospital.

We were fortunate. After being given the list of possible internal injuries and subsequent treatments for swallowing a foreign object, the vet agreed that up until then, he appeared to be showing no adverse effects. X rays were ruled out for the time being.

"You can leave him here for observation, or you can take him home and keep an eye on him. Hopefully, he will pass it."

We elected to bring him home, and although we had neither the time nor the inclination to scrutinize the situation, his normal appetite and playful activities indicated that he would need no further medical attention. The incident, however, was not without merit, because we did pay Pat more than the usual attention and discovered it was not only bobby pins, but razor blades, tweezers, small scissors, paper clips, screws, nails, and all other such small metal objects that we had to take extra care to keep out of his reach. At the sight or sound of any of the above, he was ready to pounce and grab. I can see his picture, too, in the aisle of the supermarket checkout line under the headline: "Cat Has Junkyard for a Stomach." Thankfully, his mania for metal was only a phase.

Of the four new kittens in our lives, including Lou, only Clarissa failed to thrive. She had been the weakest from the three next door, the only picky eater, who felt like no more than a feather in our hands. As the days shortened and the air chilled, a specific symptom was added to Clarissa's general poor condition. She began to have trouble breathing, serious trouble that could not be ignored. The little eyes and nose watered; she rasped and sometimes gasped for breath.

"Asthma," was the diagnosis.

"There is not much you can do other than administer a nasal spray, try to build her up, and hope for the best."

I stifled myself from asking, tongue in cheek, if she was allergic to cats!

It took time, lots of time, and hopeful patience all through the winter, but gradually the improvement came. Besides her medication, I gave Wiss what I knew howto give best—all of the TLC I could muster. Every night, I kept the soft little body close to my right side, in my arm, covered except for her beautiful face. Of course, she was in Bo's place, and since I expected some jealousy, I was grateful that Bo's nose was only slightly out of joint. In fact, her new spot brought her even closer to me, nestled on my chest with her chin resting on mine. Baby Jane parked herself on my stomach, while Red lay across my feet, Mickey, Goldie, and The Upstairs Girl were elsewhere on the bed. Pat lay nearby on another sofa.

The snow was deep that year, and each night I felt we were going into hibernation rather than merely to bed. Only the Jersey Girls did not join us. Tiffany preferred the top of a cabinet in the dining room, and Yoda was still trying to adjust to Jeannine's absence, although by that time it was approaching a year since she had gone.

I was alone in the cottage during the week. Years earlier, when my mother moved to New Bedford, Jeannine and I divided up the territory. Her domain was upstairs where she had room to expand with her evergrowing collection of clothes, TV, stereo, albums, and other paraphernalia of her generation. My domain was downstairs, where I discovered the snug comfort of a pull-out sofa, as did my furry family. One Saturday as Dicey arrived earlier than usual, he peered in the first-floor window to see all of us sleeping, Clarissa and myself underneath the green blanket, the rest in their usual spots on top.

Dicey told me later, "I thought I was looking at a swamp full of alligators."

That year, only three months after my mother died, on a stormy night in December, Mr. Benson took ill. I knew something was wrong when I saw his lights blazing into the night and he did not answer his phone. Plowing through the snow, I could hear his radio blaring; but there was no response at the door, only his poodle, Mimi, barking in recognition of my voice. Icicles obscured his door and windows. I went home, contacted his family, and before the night was over, he left for the hospital, never to return.

Good-bye, good and faithful friend. I am really alone here.

Our cottage and the one on Bay View Avenue where Madelyn used to live, as well as his own little house, were to be sold as a package. We had no desire to take on repairs, remodeling, and tenants.

"Take your time," said the executor of his estate.

"There is no hurry for you to leave."

We were being given plenty of time to regroup, make decisions. Crossroads.

The solution was to be handed us on a platter, later in the year, but for then, there was nothing we could do but wait and to take each day as it came, savoring the time that we had left in the cottage, while keeping our eyes open for a signal to indicate our next move.

The cottage was home to me from the day so many years before when I first walked inside its walls. I belonged to it in a way it would never belong to me. I never entered the door without the feeling of protective arms encircling me, calming my senses, soothing my soul. To leave it would be to leave an important part of myself. Of the new house, friends say, "It is beautiful," and I cannot dispute them. Red tones warm the natural woodwork of each room and the beamed living-room ceiling. The "white room" on the west is bright from sunlight pouring through its eight windows as plants flourish. French doors separate the large dining room from the smaller one. Yes, it is a fine house.

But despite my personal touches throughout it is not my house. All the years that we were in the cottage, we observed the comings and goings next door. Here have lived the older Goyettes, Bruno and Chris, Sylvon and Sylvia, Linda: et al, and another family, who rented it for a time, kept to themselves, whose names we never knew. The wife scolded me one night for going into "her" yard looking for Ches. Everybody's House.

I don't know when it actually started, if it had been going on all along and I was too preoccupied to notice, but while still in the cottage, more often than not, coming home in the dark, I began to question if I had forgotten to turn the lights out that morning. Living and dining room lights were only partially responsible for the yellow beams slashing the darkness and reflecting on the snow. The stairwell and kitchen lights, too, burned brightly. Surely I could not be that careless every morning. I mentioned it to friends.

"Aren't you afraid of going in there by yourself?" Never.

My suspicions were confirmed, but the mystery only halfway solved the first time I caught one of the culprits. The cats and I were all asleep when the light over the swamp suddenly flashed on. Dangling for a moment from the string-switch was none other than Baby Jane. I was still digesting this discovery when she decided to turn it off again and on again and . . . Surely the neighbors must have wondered if the place was otherwise inhabited during the hours when I was not there. A jumping kitten catching a dangling cord was understandable, but still unexplained were the lights that operated by flip switch.

Fred loves to peek around corners and is the only cat that I've ever had that could be described as sneaky and even then, only somewhat. He loves to pull little numbers and then take off the moment he is cornered. The only time he will stick around is if he thinks he is being ignored. I suspected another besides Baby Jane was involved in the Lights-On-Lights-Off game, and I was pretty sure I knew Who It Was, but I had to bide my time.

One day Fred began to run up, then down the stairs, each time down, the little nose peeking around the stairwell wall. *Act normal. Pretend you don't see him. Set him up.* I glanced ever so carefully out of the corner of my eye as I saw the paw reach around to the switch, and even though it was happening right before me, it took a moment to comprehend. He was actually flipping the switch. I made no move toward him and did not say a word. We stared into each other's eyes from across the room as the light was turned on and off and on and off.

"You little devil."

Poof. He was off. Up the stairs at top speed, waiting for me to chase him.

No, buddy. You've answered my questions. Go have your fun.

As a born and bred New Yorker, driving has never been a part of my culture, even here. Besides, my husband needed the car and garaged it in New Bedford. Tuesday was shopping night.

Never let it be questioned that good friends are like gold. Such was and is Jean Miner, who is not only a gold piece, but the kind each of us does well to find one of in a lifetime. I've been blessed to have found a few, but of them, she is certainly of the shiniest. How many Grandmothers-Who-Are-Not-Overly-Fond-of-Cats would join in the outdoor sports we allowed ourselves to be drawn into, on a weekly basis, often past 10:00 P.M.?

I could go home on any given night to be greeted in the manner normal for each cat, but grocery night was a different story. They seemed to know exactly when Mama would be arriving with those brown bags filled with goodies; and at whatever point it was that they heard me, they all flocked to the door. Jean and I devised a plan of action. Bundles left on the back steps, Jean would stand guard behind me as I eased through the door. The idea was for me to quickly squeeze in and slam it shut. After securing the cats on the front and side porches, I could bring in the bags at my leisure, as well as put away anything I didn't want them to get into. Sometimes it worked. More often than not, we were outsmarted by Baby Jane, who has the agility of a deer and the speed of lightning.

"There she goes! You on that side; I'll go over here." And the two of us would run, and turn, and dash behind the car, between the houses, from the street in the front to the one in the back. This inky butterfly would let us come within arm's length of catching her, when off she would go. Maybe we subconsciously enjoyed the exercise, or getting soaked, or sliding on the ice. Whatever the case, we never learned. Not only did we not catch her, but as soon as we stopped the chase, she would saunter over and allow herself to be picked up and cuddled, romp over, ready to go inside. If she could put it into words, I'm sure her thoughts would have been, "I guess I've given those fools enough of a workout."

It was heading toward spring when the owner of the house that Linda lived in approached us.

"You need a house. I would like to sell mine. Would you be interested?" It was a good house, larger than the cottage, though minus the porches I loved so much, with a wider, grassier yard, full of bushes and shrubs. Thus began negotiations, which were to take a few months to finalize. A chapter that had covered twenty-three years of our lives was coming to a close. That was the spring that we lost Mickey who had been there with us almost from the beginning.

And it was the summer of the storm, not a dangerous or threatening one, but dramatic for its loudness, the sharpness of its lightning, and its length. There is something mildly exciting about the approach of a thunderstorm, especially when you are in a place of safety from where you can watch, untouched, the ranting and ravings of nature. We, the cats and I, were prepared as the rumblings began, around 10:00 P.M. on a cool July night.

Good excuse to do no more chores, go to bed early, get comfortable, and enjoy the show. Each of us was cozily in our place in the swamp, lights out, when it broke. We dozed, at least I did, to awaken intermittently as the room lit up, followed by soft and sharp roars. The cats' eyes were wide; they glowed in the dark. They huddled closer and closer as we all kept warm against the faint, fresh chill from the slightly opened window.

During the hours I was awake, my senses were clear, my mind and body at rest. In the silence between the jarring noises of the thunder, which seemed to approach and recede, I allowed myself to relive it all, and those who had lived, died, and left here, those who had shared my life and my love, were remembered with a sweet ache . . . my parents, my daughter, Penny, Toodles, Fluffy . . . I would drift off and awaken. Ted, Spot, Mary, Bunny, Mick, so recently gone . . . Cuchi, Jo Jo, Little Kitty, Tina, Ches . . . and the house itself.

Good-bye. I will never stop loving you.

The storm did not abate until 8:00 A.M. It, along with my emotions, spent at last, I finally fell into a deep sleep. That night is one I will take with me wherever I go, for as long as I live.

The dread move came late in August. After papers had been signed, repairs and decorations began, lasting throughout the long and hot months. The apartment in New Bedford would no longer be feasible. Dicey and I would be together now, so in more ways than one it was to be a whole new life, for the cats as well part of the "dread," as far as the move was concerned,. Involved them. Much of our furniture in the cottage was in expensive or second hand to begin with. Not so in the apartments. It was in New Bedford that we had been able spread out in not just our place, but my mother's as well. Two different color schemes and decor needed to be combined under one roof; paintings needed to be strategically located.

And Lou to be living with my cats? She and I tolerating each other would be more than a challenge. The roomy basement, full of shelves, with enough windows for plenty of fresh air, would be home to the furniture from the cottage, as well as to the cats, all that is except Idi, who Dicey insisted would live upstairs with us and with whom Lou would have to learn to get along. As it turned out, she never did more than spit at him as she passed by.

I had always heard how cats cannot accept a new house, as indeed, had been the case with Ches. So, it was with apprehension that I brought Bo over to test the waters, so to speak. Bo has a way of turning her head almost completely around, then staring into my eyes with her big ones as she holds to me tighter than ever. That is how it was when I brought her over to inspect our new home. She looked all around in interest and excitement, but only from the security of my arms or my lap. Though wide-eyed with curiosity, she did not have enough to explore on her own. After a few minutes of claws digging into my shoulders and knees, I said, "Bo, we can do this at home."

So, when the Big Day arrived, it amazed me to see her immediate recognition and familiarity with the place. There was no strangeness; in fact, as I brought them all over, one by one, each made an immediate and total adjustment, as though this was a most normal happening. Only Idi cried and trembled, but this was just for the few moments spent outdoors. And Goldie, too, was stressed enough to leave a damp circle on my shirt.

But once established in their new quarters, for all anyone knew, they could have been living there for years. No longer able to sit in any window they chose, their need for sunshine and fresh air was resolved when we had a screen house built into the east side of the house into which they can enter and leave at will, through a cellar window with a sliding door. An added bonus is the grass they have access to. Not the same as at the cottage, but that is what change is all about. For one freedom lost, another was gained.

Only Lou is allowed the run of the big yard, and then, only with Dicey, and only because she obeys him. Notwithstanding her nastiness, I will give it to her for being obedient. She will follow to the letter every instruction that Dicey gives her, whether it be to "come here," "go in the other room," "sit on this chair," or "get into the house." Since acquiring Lou, Dicey had come a long way in understanding the makeup of cats, but still he gave credit for intelligence only to her. That is why I was so surprised one evening when I had worked a little later and called to say I was on my way home, to hear from Dicey that "Lou is missing."

Home, he gave me the full story—as far as it went. Earlier, Lou had been out in the yard with him. He told her to go in; and the last he saw of her. She was heading for the front door. Nowhere to be found in the house. He probably did not follow her in soon enough. She must have gone out again to find him. He had stopped to chat with the man next door, a landlord who lived on the other side of the Neck. But where was she? What was so unusual was that Lou in not a roamer. To the contrary, she has made it a habit never to be more than a few feet away from Dicey; self-sufficient she was certainly was not.

Our search was methodical, Dicey going to the end of the street, I to the immediate neighbors. Backyards, drive-ways, sheds, garages were searched: our eyes peeled as we looked upward into heavily laden branches. Doors were knocked on, people questioned, and every few minutes as we met and compared notes, we assured each other that surely she would be waiting for us on the steps at home.

That night we combed the beach, all the way around to the far side of the cove, along the row of houses where Mary Boy used to live. Next, together, down one end of the avenue to the Public Landing and the Yacht Club on Hingham Bay; down the hill on the other end, through the swamp and the boatyard, around to Perry Beach on Quincy Bay. It was deep into the night before we returned home, heartsick and exhausted. My fear was that someone had snatched her up, although why they would want her was beyond my wildest guess. There are few things sadder than to see a strong man, a man's man cry. Dicey's devastation was complete.

No matter how anxious we were for her return, we could not stay home from work to look for Lou, but the second night we were well supplied with copies of a flyer with her picture and the promise of a reward for her return. By then, we figured that she had been frightened by something, a dog, a loud noise, and had run clear of the neighborhood. By the time we collapsed in bed, all two hundred flyers had been distributed, with the help of some local teenagers.

By the third night, we tried to accept what we could not change. Besides our own efforts, we had put a flyer in all the local stores, as well as an ad in the newspaper and on cable TV's lost-and-found. No stone left unturned, we could do no more but to get on with our own lives.

The September air was warm, and as Dicey played the organ, I left the front door open as I stood in front of the house facing the bay. I still brought a flashlight with me when I went out in the dark, "just in case" a rustle in the bushes might be Lou. I pointed it up into the tall trees where squirrels slept in hollows, in groups of two and three, opening their little eyes at the intruding light. I began to silently pray, the only sound the music drifting from the house. I called once—"Spooky" and thought it only my imagination when I heard what sounded like the snap of a limb. "Spooky" again. Another snap. It came from the area right next to our fence. Immediately on the other side of our quince bush was the window of our neighbor's garage. Was I seeing things, or was that a little white patch?

I nearly screamed into Dicey, "Shut that thing off and come out here! I think I've found Lou."

It was she, all right, frantically signaling me from her prison. It was 12:30 A.M. This situation was going to be embarrassing. First, we had to awaken the tenant, who gave us the landlord's telephone number, then we had to explain our dilemma. Yes, he would come— happily. He understood. Necker's are not just a special people. As this world goes, they have no match. Now it was easy to figure out what had happened. A couple of days earlier, when Lou had gone into the house, she likely heard Dicey talking to this man and came out again to investigate. This time, she ran into his garage, which he evidently closed and locked soon 'thereafter. The mystery was why she had not come to the window when we first looked in there and called her., Dicey was so excited that I ended up being the one to pick her up and carry her into the house—and to feed her.

When she wants something, such as piece of bacon or chicken, Lou knows how to be "the sweetest piece of bacon or chicken. Lou knows how to be "the sweetest pussycat in" the world," and this she was for at least five minutes. As soon as her hunger was satisfied I might have guessed, she turned and spit at me.

When winter came, we lost our dear Goldie, and Yoda followed in the spring. Both gave us little warning. Goldie was rasping on a Thursday night, ever louder by Friday. After a weekend in the hospital, the vet called me at work on Monday morning.

"She has throat cancer that is so advanced we cannot understand how she has lived this long. I suggest we put her to sleep now, while she is under anesthesia."

I could do nothing but give my consent and cry my heart out. "Kiss her for me, please." "I will," said the male voice.

Yoda showed no sign of being ill. She just stopped eating. She, too, was hospitalized for two days. Again we received the news by phone.

"I am so sorry. We found nothing to be wrong with her. She just died."

We were saddened but not really surprised. We had been informed years earlier that cats with her physical defects do not live very long. She had had a bad start in her little life, but it was made up to her all along, and we were grateful to have had her for five of her eight years.

The next January, Idi Amin died peacefully at home, of old age.

It was the previous July, when I made one of those innocent, offhand remarks that we are all capable of making at any time, to anyone, not for a moment thinking it to be something we may never live down. I don't even know why I said it. I certainly did not mean it, though I don't believe I've yet been able to convince Dicey. The words I have learned to never again utter to my husband: "I wish I had a new baby to raise."

Whatever nostalgia or foolhardiness brought on the mood, at least he had the good sense to know what kind of baby the mother of a thirty-one-year-old did not mean. He looked at me, I quickly added, "forget it," and assumed he had done just that. I know I did, until one week later.

We had been out for a drive in the country. It was enjoyable for a little while, but I was restless and anxious to get home. A friend was with us and asked if we might take a few extra minutes to explore a nearby lake that brought back her childhood memories of camp. Dicey was enthusiastic; I was resigned. Perhaps if we had been home, the "surprise" we found waiting for us could have been forestalled, or at least deprived of its mystery.

I'm not sure which of us opened the unlocked door to the back porch first, or who was more surprised.

"Joyce, I would never have believed you would stoop this low to have your way."

While reeling from this verbal slap, I looked more closely at the object of his accusation, and, of course, my reaction only contributed to his suspicions.

"Tina. It looks like Tina."

Not really, I concluded, when I examined the long-legged black male kitten, but certainly my first glance had been heart-stopping for a moment. Where he came from, was anybody's guess, but my husband was sure that he knew.

"You said you wanted one. You probably thought I would say no,' so you took matters in your own hands. You arranged for somebody to drop him here. That's why you wanted to go for a ride. "

"No, Dicey, Your memory is short. I am the one who wanted to come home, but was out-voted. I did not want to go out in the first place. "

My words were weightless. I don't believe he even heard me.

"It isn't the cat; it's the deceit. Do you realize that you've never lied to me before? "

My protests were useless, but one fact remained. The kitten was not going to be turned back out onto the street the way I was turned out of the bedroom. Lou would have Dicey all to herself for the next three nights while the kitten and I camped out on the living-room sofa.

No one knew, of course, where he had come from, or if they did, they were keeping it to themselves. We, or I should say, I, half-expected a confession in the form of a follow-up phone call. Something.

Anything...

"I thought it was yours...." or "I knew you wouldn't mind taking another one."

Someone had seen him wandering farther down Bay View Avenue the day before. Beyond that— nothing.

Dicey and I had too many mundane things to say to each other. He could not keep silent indefinitely.

After about a week, "Well, you've got your wish.

What are you going to name him?" "I think he looks like a 'Spike.' "

"What does a 'Spike' look like?"

"Long and lean and gangling," which was how our newest addition was growing.

I suggested that he be put downstairs with the rest of "my" cats. Spike has a noise he makes in his throat when he wants it known he will not go along with the program. Plan A discarded, we wondered how he could possibly survive in Lou's territory. It is true that wonders never cease.

Rather than regarding him as a rival, Spike became her very first playmate. Occasionally, one of them will nip a bit too hard when they are wrestling, but by far their behavior is closer to that of any two normal kittens raised together. If Lou were a child, I would be declaring that she is human after all. This, despite the fact that Spike did not take long to decide that he, too, is Dicey's cat. He is very loving with me until my husband comes home, at which time I may as well cease to exist. Like any boy, he likes to play rough, and to a point Dicey will oblige him.

"I am afraid I will trip on him."

It is true that he is never far from Dicey's feet in waking hours and wraps around his legs as they sleep. Lou watches from the top of the dresser. She has even learned to be slightly more tolerant of me.

Spike was with us for, perhaps, a day when the porch on which he was deposited became off-limits to other animals, even people. The postman questioned Dicey, "Did you teach your cat to growl at me?"

I was not home when it happened, but Dicey was as excited as a kid who had hit a home run and won his team's game.

"Did you ever see a singing cat?" *No, not redly.*

Dicey had been singing in the shower when he heard a strange nose. Shower curtain aside, there was Spike sitting on the edge of the sink, trying with all his heart to harmonize with his papa.

Or maybe he was asking Dicey to quiet it down.

I hope it happens again someday, when I am there.

His name needed enhancing, and this was provided for us by the late night talk shows and entertainment segments of the "News." He seemed to be the man of the hour, and I don't even remember if he was being interviewed or just talked about, but it seemed that on every channel we turned to for a spell there, the name heard most frequently repeated was .

There is no question that my wish had been granted. Like it or not, I had been given a new baby to raise, and his name was Spike Lee.

Going Home

Yes, I dream of the past, and I'm sure I always will. I wouldn't want to let it go, since some of it is as much a part of me as my own skin. But it will all grow dimmer in time, especially as dreams of the future come into clearer focus. I have one now that has been with me for about a year.

"You want to go WHERE?" "That's right."-

"Pipe dreaming," my husband calls it. "Nothing you really want to do— a phase you are going through."

It started on the weekend that he received an award for long-ago accomplishments in the field of music, and I, too, thought it would not last. Will it come true? Will it ever really happen? I don't know but do you know how it is when you want something so badly you believe with every fiber of your being that it's just got to happen?

The scenario is so clear that I can almost reach out and touch it.

It is October. The air itself is filled with excitement and tingles as if washed with champagne. We have hired a limousine for the occasion. The orange sky of the west fades into a deep purple. In the distance we catch a glimpse of the towers of Lower Manhattan. Graceful bridges hang like diamond necklaces.

We cross the 138th Street bridge and turn left into Manhattan and on down Fifth Avenue. There it is ahead of us and to our right—Central Park cloaked in darkness, hiding we know not what. It is L'Heure Bleue— the Blue Hour. Lights twinkle, taxis honk. We are caught up in the heart-beat of The City That Never Sleeps.

The fantasy has not gone any further, so I do not yet know where, uptown or down, eastside or west, but somewhere a house is waiting for us. Someday, after it has been renovated, it will be known as DJ's House of Cats a uniquely designed B and B for those travelers who miss tin, cat(s) they cannot bring with them—who would have the option of sharing their bed with a furry friend . . . but for now, soft lamplight gleams in welcome from the many-paned windows. Lit candles cast their flickering shadows against dark wood panels. A decadent cheesecake sits on the sideboard. Someone is in the kitchen. Two Long Island ducklings are roasting in the oven, one for us and one for them, and the pungent scent of the orange sauce mingles with the late roses adorning the warm rooms, to tickle our senses even as we reach the doorstep.

There is a stained-glass entryway for me, a piano for Dicey, a hearth for Spooky, a plump pillow for Bo. Pat and Fred will play in a city garden, enclosed with brick walls, covered with ivy and steeped in enchantment.

The ocean will no longer be at our feet, but there are the rivers—the meandering East and the mighty Hudson. Farther on the horizon, the hills of Staten Island guard the gateway to the Atlantic.

In the limo, Fred, Pat, and The Upstairs Girl are sitting upright, one on each side, one between us. Clarissa and Baby Jane, our little chorus girls, are stretched out in the rear window, already little New Yorkers, oblivious to their surroundings, queens of all they survey. After whimpering for the best part of the trip, Tiffany is at last quiet. Lou is sleeping like a baby in Dicey's arms. Bo has not shifted from her position in my lap since we left the Neck, a few hours and a lifetime behind us.

Only Spike Lee is walking around, looking out first one window, then another, not wanting to miss a sight or sound. His Aunt Joanne has come along to give us a hand until getting settled. She remarks what a good boy he was here, and I nod in agreement.

I indulge in foolishness that belongs only in dreams.

"Look, Spikey, there's the park. Tomorrow we will put a leash on you and take you for a walk. It's been a long journey that's lasted for many years; but, my loves, your mama is home."

And if my ears could reach beyond the sweetly familiar noise of the city I know they would hear the message being passed from one alley to the next, from Harlem to the Battery:

"Pssst. . She's back!"

Gallery

Lou and her Daddy

Spot & Maryanne
napping with Nana

Mary Anne and Spot
with Nana

Spot

Spot

Jo Jo's Family

Bunny on Patrol

Bo & Goldie

Bo Elizabeth and Goldie

Kitten Bo Elizabeth

Cuchi

Mickey saying his prayers

www.ingramcontent.com/pod-product-compliance
Lightning Source LLC
Chambersburg PA
CBHW071400120626
46546CB00002B/762